THE HISTORY OF THE

SENECA INDIANS

ALVIN H. DEWEY

THE HISTORY OF THE

SENECA INDIANS

by

ARTHUR C. PARKER

EMPIRE STATE HISTORICAL PUBLICATION XLIII

IRA J. FRIEDMAN, INC.
Port Washington, Long Island, N. Y.

THE HISTORY OF THE SENECA INDIANS

Originally Published in 1926
Reissued in 1967 by Ira J. Friedman, Inc.

Library of Congress Catalog Card No: 67-16256

EMPIRE STATE HISTORICAL PUBLICATIONS SERIES XLIII

CONTENTS.

ILLUSTRATIONS.

TEXT CUTS.

FOREWORD.

For many years there has been an insistent demand for a short history of the Seneca Indians, the former lords of the Genesee Country. In general, Morgan's "League of the Iroquois" has been the principal guide, but its pages embrace more of ethnology than of history. Most of the shorter sketches that have appeared have failed to set forth the underlying causes of tribal action and to give the Seneca people a setting that would explain the phenomena of their folk-ways. There is, therefore, a need to be met and satisfied. This, we have attempted in this resume.

The manuscript files of the author are filled with many obscure references, and his own notes, taken on the Indian reservations during the past quarter century, embrace facts never published. It was from this file, and from its "index rerum" that the account presented in "The History of the Genesee Country," edited by Lockwood R. Doty, published by the S. J. Clarke Publishing Company of Chicago (1925), was compiled. In writing the present account, the same outline has been used, which will account for certain sequences of paragraphs and similarities of expression, but having written both accounts, the author may be excused for not quoting his own utterances.

It is hoped that this brief paper may provide an easily read and readily accessible account of the people to whom America owes so much. We have shown herein that the partisanship of the Iroquois saved for an English-speaking race the control of the Middle-Atlantic area. There can be no question of this, for the power of France would have grown so naturally and so effectively, that had it not been for the hostility of the Iroquois, France would have controlled Canada, New York, and Ohio, and have established a route up the Mississippi, which would have tied together the two regions. With this penetration, the English would have been displaced, and even if their colonists had found small and protected locations, a well-established body of French colonists would have made difficult the consolidation of the British colonies, and therefore prevented the later rise of the United States.

More than this, the resistance offered by the Eastern Indians had much to do with the crystallization of American character. The colonist was forced to dwell along the·coast and east of the Alleghanies. A continental penetration was made difficult by the interior Indians, thus preventing the migrations of bands of European settlers, bent on establishing independent colonies and states of their own. But for this there might have been here a Swedish state, a Spanish sub-kingdom, a French colony, a Dutch republic, several English dominions, and perhaps a negro kingdom. The resistance of the red man, however, kept the European pent in a zone wherein he developed a national consciousness.

When the Revolutionary War had freed the American colonists and the states were established, this reservoir of European blood rose high against its barrier. It burst the dam and flowed westward over a continent. Obstructions were swept aside and, like a flood, it spread westward to the Pacific. Thus spread the American people over their continental expanse. They moved as a single people, speaking one language, loyal to one flag, determined to have but one country, and one magnificent national ideal.

In the crystallizing of these forces of development, the red man had an important and even essential part. We must credit him as being a peculiarly constructive

factor in American history, and look upon his aggrava-
tions as we look upon the pangs of birth. No nation is
truly great which has not emerged from a crisis, and
which never knew resistance.

In the history of this struggle of a race to protect
its homeland, we have shown how the Seneca reacted to
the conflicting and perplexing events about him, and
we have shown in the end how the Seneca people
became the loyal allies of the nation that arose, all
powerful, upon their ancient domain. And even the
Seneca has preserved himself in crisis, emerging from
his own cultural state to that which the white man has
provided. He has resisted the French, the Dutch, the
English and the encroachments of the American
republic, and today forms the largest nation of Indian
people in the East still remaining in its ancient homeland.

As New York's most persistent red men, we have
therefore set forth their remarkable story, in the hope
that on this Tenth Anniversary of Morgan Chapter, and
of Alvin H. Dewey's presidency, our Association may
have another aid in comprehending the archeology, the
ethnology and the Indian history of the Empire State.

ARTHUR C. PARKER.

Municipal Museum, Rochester, N. Y.

INTRODUCTION.

The Genesee Country lies west of a line dropped due south from Sodus Bay on Lake Ontario. It is the region of Western New York, and one of the most attractive and fertile in the entire United States. Climatically, it lies in the isothermal zone characterized by the world's most vigorous and resourceful people.

Nature seems to have saved this region for special purposes, and the hand that guides the destiny of nations held back settlement by Europeans until after the Revolutionary War. Until 1812, this region was largely a wilderness, with only a few settlements of any great size. Buffalo was then a struggling village of less than 2,000 souls, Batavia had a population of about 3,000, and Canandaigua was an important place of 1,000 and, indeed, practically the Capital of the region. Rochester had just been projected, and a single log cabin had been built. No one dreamed that it would grow into a thriving city of its present population and area. It was then a mud hole by the river, and its miasmatic swamps and woods were filled with bears, wolves, wildcats, rattlesnakes, and mosquitoes.

Yet, since pioneer days, the Genesee Country has blossomed and become one of Earth's fairest regions. The Ridge road, the bridge across the Genesee built in 1812-13, the Erie Canal, built in 1821, and then the railroads, built in the 50's, provided the way by which travelers might reach Rochester, cross the Genesee and find here an abiding place.

But those who find this region a dwelling place incomparable must remember that another race, and another nation, once dwelt here and loved it fully as well. Their campfires now are only ashes.

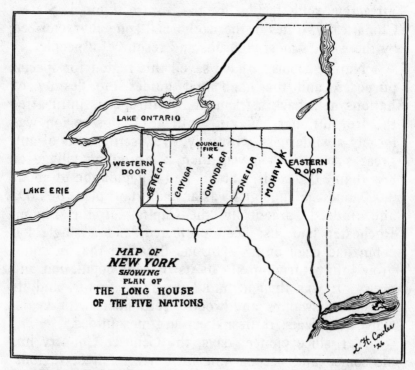

Fig. 1. This diagram shows the relative position of the five Iroquois nations and graphically explains why the confederacy of tribes called itself, "the long house".

Plate 2. Typical Seneca of 1800. This picture is from a water color by W. A. McKenna, owned by Frank L. Reuss of Albany. It is painted from the Morgan plate.

I. ABORIGINAL INHABITANTS.

The Genesee Country is commonly spoken of as the land of the Seneca, and as a matter of fact, the Seneca still retain small, reserved tracts that they call their own, in the valleys of the Tonawanda, the Cattaraugus and the Alleghany. They have given up forever all the land in the valley of the Genesee and the country to the east of it, but so deeply impressed upon this region is the former presence of these indigenes that the names they left behind for stream, river, lake and village are still retained to enrich our geographical nomenclature. The very name *Genesee* is from their language.

The Seneca Homeland. This Genesee homeland was a land they loved, and poignant was the regret when they left it, and retreated to sequestered spots further toward the sunset. To them it was a holy land where the bones of their ancestors were buried, and where their nation dwelt in the height of its glory. For many years,—even to this day,—the Seneca wander back over these hallowed spots to dream again of the days when their nation was a power with which nations reckoned. Yet, today when they come in their automobiles to camp on our hillsides and in our glens we know them not, for like the landscape, they too have changed their dress.

Yet the Seneca were not the first to roam this region. Other tribes had their camps and villages here, and even mighty nations had their council fires along the streams and upon the hills.

1. The Algonkian Occupation.

Algonkian Periods. It is difficult to say what people first lived here,* whether the archaic Algonkian

---

*The differentiation of these cultures, particularly the successive stages of culture, was first set forth in my work, "The Archeological History of New York," published by the State Museum.

or the Eskimo-like people. It is certain that the Algonkian tribes came very early, and it is equally true that some northern people with implements like the Eskimo roamed the hills and upper terraces. Then came the second period or intermediate Algonkian tribes. These people began to use crude pottery which they made from local clays, although to some extent they still used steatite or soap stone dishes, as did their predecessors. The third period Algonkian tribes spread in every direction throughout the Genesee Country, for they seem to have been a numerous people. They were bold and busy hunters and well acquainted with the arts of the forest. While they roamed afar, they also had settled villages and fields of corn and beans. Their flint workers were expert, and many of the finest specimens of chipped flint, jasper and chalcedony must be credited to them. They were makers of grooved axes, roller pestles, notched choppers and hoes, gouges, beveled adzes, gorgets, bird stones, banner stones, bone implements (as harpoons and awls), and a well developed type of pottery decorated over its entire surface with the impression of cords or imitations of cord markings.

These people had an abundance of life's necessities, but were frugal. They did not waste their artifacts like the later Iroquois, and for this reason they did not write their history so deeply in the soil. Nevertheless, they present ample evidence of having lived here for an extended period of time. It seems quite likely that the various Algonkian occupations of western New York cover an era of more than 5,000 years and perhaps nearly twice as long, for as we enter the archaic period, artifacts become rarer, and many are found deep in the soil.

The Algonkian tribes of various periods and cultures did not hold this region undisputed, for again and again other stocks intruded and gained footholds for periods of time, greater or less. Among the strange people who came were those who in certain phases of culture resembled the Eskimo. They made broad, crudely chipped arrowpoints, semi-lunar choppers and double edged, rubbed slate knives or spears. We do not know when they came, but we can place them somewhere between the advent of the archaic Algonkins and the second Algonkian period, though they may have preceded all comers. Investigation alone can decide.

A New Culture. At some stage in the third Algonkian period a new cultural influence began to manifest itself. It apparently came from the west or south-west. The people who brought it were builders of mounds and they brought with them a new appreciation of finely made articles of stone. They brought copper implements, monitor pipes and polished implements and articles of green-banded slate, such as outcrops in Ohio. They made large shell beads and cut disks from iridescent shells, and they used the bannerstone, the birdstone and gorget. Apparently, they did not build stockaded fortifications, or, if they did, very few were set in walled bases of earth.

Who these people were, we do not know. They may have been an Ohioan-Algonkian people or they may have been of some other stock, as Siouan. Their methods of interment were various. When they buried in mounds they sometimes walled up the burial with slabs of stone, as at Napoli, Poland Center and Squawkie Hill. In some of the stoned-up graves have been found finely made stone tubes, some of them filled with a curious black powder. Again, not all the walled graves are in mounds. Where individual graves are found, or groups of them, the same sort of artifacts are discovered. At Vine Valley on Canandaigua Lake, in 1922, were found more than thirty graves of this culture and

careful notes made describing them. Among the implements from this site are awls of bone and antler, copper
celts, copper nails or rivets, shell beads, birdstones, a
bone bar amulet, bola stones, and several gorgets. One
of these shows plain evidence of having been made with
precision, the ends being arcs of circles, the centers of
which are the holes in the gorget.

2. The Mound Builders.

The Mound Culture. From the evidence furnished
by the sites of the Genesee Country alone, not to
mention the testimony of other localities, we are war-
ranted in stating that the so-called Mound Builders
were no more than energetic Indian tribes, who during
a period of peace were able to develop their native arts.
There is no evidence whatsoever of any mysterious race
with a "higher civilization" that has been blotted out
by the later Indians,—at least in the sense that the
mound building tribes were not Indians themselves.
There is nothing that the "Mound Builders" had or did
that the Indians did not have and do, for, indeed, all were
Indians. If we wish to pursue the subject further, we
will find accounts of French and Spanish explorers who
actually saw Indians building mounds. Our earlier
antiquarians, lacking information, built up strange
theories that later investigation proved erroneous.

In the popular mind the Mound Builders still remain
in an entertaining myth, but American anthropologists
long ago branded the theory of a separate people as a
fable, shelving it along with the story of tempered
copper, the Israelitish origin of the Indians, Atlantis and
the making of arrowheads by heating flint and dropping
on water. In the light of new discoveries it may be
heartless to spoil our "fairy tales," but facts are not
entirely devoid of romance, and truth affords the more

Plate 3. An Algonkian pottery vessel from near Auburn.

solid satisfaction of being a stable foundation for further structures.

3. The Tribes of the Iroquois.

At some point during the height of the third Algonkian period, and at a time when the mound culture still prevailed, another group began to enter this region. They were a distinctive people with habits, tastes and prejudices all their own. More than this they were a people of greater mental energy than had heretofore occupied the region. It may be that they were less apt in some of the material arts, but their skill took other directions. They were a persistent people of great ingenuity and possessed the racial will to persevere in their desires until they conquered. They were the Iroquois,—the Men of Men, as they called themselves.

Origin of the Iroquois. Some early historians, basing their statements upon an account of the shifting of the Mohawk, have tried to make us believe that the Iroquoian tribes came out of the north from the region about the mouth of the St. Lawrence, but when we have examined the evidences afforded by archeology and ethnology, we will find all the facts against this belief. The Iroquoian people came from the west and south-west, and not from the north, if archeology and ethnology are to be relied upon. Their roots lay in the agricultural southlands.

The Iroquois Stock. When we speak of "the Iroquois" we mean the group of tribes that afterward became the Five Nations Confederacy, sometimes called the League of the Iroquois. But the Iroquoian stock itself included a much larger group of linguistically related people. In the north, between Georgian Bay and the St. Lawrence, and southward along the northern shores of Lake Ontario, were the Huron-Wyandot tribes; in the Niagara peninsulas, on both sides of the river,

were the tribes and allies of the Neutrals or Atti-
wendaronks; southward of Lake Erie and extending
down the Alleghany, and between it and the territory of
the Conestoga tribes, was the land of the Erie, a populous tribe; along the Susquehanna to its mouth were
the several tribes of the Conestoga, and Susquehannock;
in the south, in the hills of the Carolinas and westward
into Tennessee, were the divisions of the Cherokee, and
further east in North Carolina were the Tuscarora, the
Nottaway and the Meherrin. All these tribes were surrounded by other stocks; in the north by the Algonkian,
in the south by the Muskhogean and Siouan. The Iroquoian linguistic stock was not wide spread, and everywhere it was hemmed in by hostile and alien peoples.
It was distributed in three great geographical groups,
for the innate genius of the Iroquois, they would have
been destroyed either by themselves through internal
strife or by their unrelenting outside foes. They were
to the great disadvantage of its own blood kinsmen. But
through Illinois,—where they began a north-eastward
journey along the Great Lakes.

One or two large groups pressed southward again
and the alliances of its constituent tribes were frequently
between the millstones of the gods; when there
was no grist, they ground upon themselves, to their
doom.

4. Migration of the Iroquois.

Archeological evidence points out the movement of
the Iroquoian tribes from some mid-Mississippi valley
point, perhaps beyond the mouth of the Ohio in
Arkansas. Here, they were in contact with the Caddo
and the Sioux. We know not what started the migration, but groups of Iroquoian tribes began to push up
the Ohio, and others still further up the Mississippi,—
perhaps to the mouth of the Missouri, thence overland

and traversed the Alleghanies, to occupy its foothills
and the valleys to the east. These, sub-dividing, became
the Cherokee divisions. Others pushed southward along
Lake Erie, and still others crossed the Detroit to occupy
the region between Lake Huron on the west, Lakes
Erie and Ontario on the south, and thence along the
St. Lawrence valley nearly to the mouth of the river.

The tribes that pushed across the Detroit later drew
together and respectively formed the Huron-Wyandot,
the Neutral and the Mohawk-Onondaga groups. Those
who chose to push along the south side of Lake Erie
and move across Ohio became the Erie, the Conestoga
and the Seneca. One of the northern groups pushed
across the Alleghanies or down the Susquehanna to
form the Tuscarora tribes. Other smaller divisions split
off as time went on.

There was a well developed spirit of race pride
among these people, and they called themselves the
Ongweh Howeh, meaning Surpassing Men, Men of Men,
and the Most Truly Human Race. They believed themselves the "chosen people" and acted accordingly.

5. The Neutral Nation.

Among the tribes along the lakes was a most
important one, called the Attiwendaronk or Neutral
Nation, so named because it would not wage war upon
any of its kins-people. Just why this was so we have
no sure means of knowing, but we may at least conjec-
ture that it was because within the Neutral Nation, and
ruling a portion of it, was a woman known as "the Mother
of Nations," sometimes called "the peace queen". According to Iroquois tradition, the original Mother of
Nations was a woman called Djikonsaseh, the first
woman born on earth. Her eldest daughter was her
successor, so that the line came down in perpetuity. She
was the arbiter of peace, and the nation in which she

dwelt must preserve peace with all the brother nations that had grown from the great mother's brood. Thus the Neutral Nation occupied both the western and eastern peninsulas of the Niagara, having many towns on the west side of the Niagara and four large villages on the east side, one of which was the capital of the nation, wherein dwelt the great mother. This capital in early historic times was at Ga-yen-no-gah (Kienuka), on the Niagara escarpment above Lewiston and on the boundary of the present Tuscarora reservation. It was America's first Peace Court, and the first Hague, and its location was not ill-chosen as a "city of refuge".

The Neutral were sedentary village-dwellers and had large fields of corn, beans, squashes, melons and other garden produce. There is little doubt that the earth-works in northern Erie county and in Genesee, Orleans and Wyoming counties were built by them, but by far the greater number of their works are across the Niagara in the Province of Ontario. The double circle fortification near Shelby was probably theirs, as was the great work at Oakfield.

The Neutral Nation has a melancholy history, and one of great interest to those who look for romance in the annals of races. The French missionaries, pushing their way down the St. Lawrence, heard of the Neutrals, and as early as 1626 the Franciscan friar, LaRoche, Dallion, visited their villages and began to make converts. He was followed by Fathers Brebeuf and Chaumonot, who established missions among them. For a considerable time they were the concern of the valiant Catholic priests, who braved the forests for the sake of saving the souls of men. Eventually, as we shall see, the Neutral Nation was destroyed. The year 1651 saw the end of these people as a distinct nation, and just why, we shall discover later when we trace the rise of the Iroquois League.

Plate 4. An Iroquoian pottery vessel. Mohawk valley type.

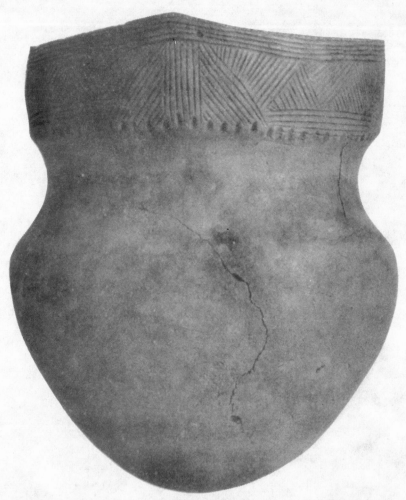

Plate 5. A typically Iroquoian pottery vessel, found at 212th Street, New York City. It is mute evidence of the influence of the Iroquois in Algonkian centers. From a photograph by the American Museum of Natural History.

6. The Erie.

The Jesuit priests in their *Relations* tell of another tribe, and lingered to see its downfall and to describe it. This tribe was the Erie or the Cat. It was a powerful group of people with the common Iroquoian features in its organization. Its domain stretched from the region of the Neutral and south of it, along the Cattaraugus to the Alleghany, thence along the waterways and valleys far inland from Lake Erie, and extending through western Pennsylvania and northern Ohio. The Huron people of the north, from whom they probably separated, called them Yenresh, and from this the name Erie is derived. It means "long tailed" and probably alludes to the robes of panther skin worn over their heads and shoulders by these people. The Seneca called them Jigonsasehónoh, or the People of the Fat Face, this term referring to the wild cat, The Jesuits hearing this term frequently called them *Nation du Chat* (Nation of the Cat).

The Erie tribes occupied a portion of the land once held by the mound-building tribes, and, indeed, with the Seneca, may have absorbed some of these extirpated people. We know from archeological research that the earlier Erie pottery sometimes resembled that of the Ohio mounds, and that their pipes of stone frequently were identical in form. Erie villages* and camps, fortifications and corn fields covered many parts of Chautauqua county, extended through Cattaraugus, Allegany and Wyoming and even into Erie, Warren, McKean and Potter counties in Pennsylvania, thence westward through northern Ohio, where one important site is located on Conneaut creek.

The writer has examined scores of Erie village sites and fortifications throughout this region and has dug

---

*Vide, Parker, "An Erie Indian Village and Burial Site," Bulletin 117, N. Y. State Museum.

deep into the graves after their buried records. The numerous earth-works along Clear creek in Chautauqua county are theirs, the site at Ripley excavated in 1906 was a stronghold of the Erie, the hilltop defences in Cattaraugus county are the result of their efforts, as perhaps are some of the forts along the upper Genesee in Allegany county. These groan for scientific examination, but the amateur must not touch them until he is schooled and trained to make his records and place them in the archives of reputable institutions.

Like the Neutral, the Erie had a tragic history, and it was brought to a closing chapter by their Iroquois neighbors who lived east of them across the Genesee. The Jesuits' record of their passing is as vivid a chapter as we may find in the entire *Relations*. (1655-'56).

7. The Huron Tribes.

Before proceedng further we should crystalize our understanding of the Huron to the north, for their alliances had much to do with the trend of history. The fate of the Genesee country hinges upon their movements; indeed, so does the story of the European invasion and occupation.

The people whom Cartier found along the St. Lawrence in 1534-43, were the northeastern Huron, or Wyandot (Wendat). He recorded that these people were engaged in combat with another people living south of them, whom they described as cruel and war-like, and called Trudamani and Agouionda, meaning "they who attack us". The later Champlain mentions these enemies of the Huron, and Lescarbot, in 1603 in his *Nova Francia*, writes of the destruction of the Huron people along the St. Lawrence by the Iroquois, whom he says appeared "to the number of 8,000 men, and discomfited all their enemies whom they surprised in their enclosures". Thus, at this early date, we have an account of the Huron-Iroquois war,—a war of great

significance in history.   The fate of North America was
decided by this war, and it resulted eventually in giving
England supremacy over France.

Divisions of the Huron.   The Huron were a confederated group of four independent tribes and several
smaller divisions.   The *Relations of* 1639 give the
names of these tribes as the Attignaouantan or *Bear
People*, the Attigneeongnahac or *Cord People*, the
Arendahronon, *Rock People*, and the Tohontaenrat or
White Fared or *Deer People*.   The non-affiliated tribes
were the *Bowl People*, Ataronchronon and the later
Wenroh People,— refugees from Iroquois wrath.   The
Bear and the Cord people were the oldest and most
influential, and they gave refuge to the Rock and Deer
people in the latter part of the 16th century, about 1590
to 1600.   For political reasons and for mutual safety,
a confederation seems to have been formed, an organization to which Huron government was particularly
adapted.   It is the incorporation of the Rock with the
Deer people, and their migration from the St. Lawrence
valley to the region between Lake Huron and the Bay
of Quinte, which has caused some early historians to
believe that all the Iroquois people came down from the
north,—as if they might not have gone north, and then
moved south and westward again,—which is precisely
what happened.   The Hurons consolidated, and the
Mohawk-Onondagas crossed the St. Lawrence to occupy
the lands to the south.   The coming of the eastern
Iroquois (the Mohawk-Oneida-Onondaga group), into
New York is comparatively recent.

The Huron people were sedentary and agricultural.
Their palisaded villages were numerous and populous.
The fortified towns were surrounded by triple palisades,
from 16 to 35 feet high, having fighting platforms running entirely around the inside.   Upon these were piled
stones, arms and baskets of water with which to

extinguish fire, should it ignite from the enemy's fire-arrows. These tribes were grouped in the general Iroquois system of clans, and women had a large share in government, possessing the sole right to nominate the civil chiefs, from hereditary groups of eligible candidates.

French Influence. With the coming of the French, missions were established and many converts were made, though not without much opposition from the native priesthood. Nevertheless, the Huron chiefs, perceiving the advantage of a cordial contact with the French, and fearing their enmity, frequently encouraged, and even invited, the ministrations of the missionary Fathers. Religion thus was made the serving maid of shrewd politics. Nor is the reason obscure: the advantages of trade and the desire to enlist powerful allies against the Iroquois to the south were sufficient. At the very beginning of the contact the Huron poured into the ears of Champlain the story of Iroquois aggression and enlisted his aid. Thus on July 6, 1609, Champlain, with two French soldiers armed with guns and with 60 Huron allies, attacked 200 Mohawks at Ticonderoga. This was the first Iroquois experience with fire arms, and, astonished by the execution of the guns, they quickly gave way, in terrorized flight. In 1610, there was another battle in which the Iroquois resisted most valiantly, but in the end nearly 100 perished. Five years later (1615) came the expedition against the Onondaga, but Champlain only reached one of the large Oneida strongholds. This he failed to take, and returned wounded and disgusted.

8. The Huron-Iroquois War.

Let us now consider just what the French were doing in attacking the Iroquois. True, they were punishing the people who harassed them at every turn,

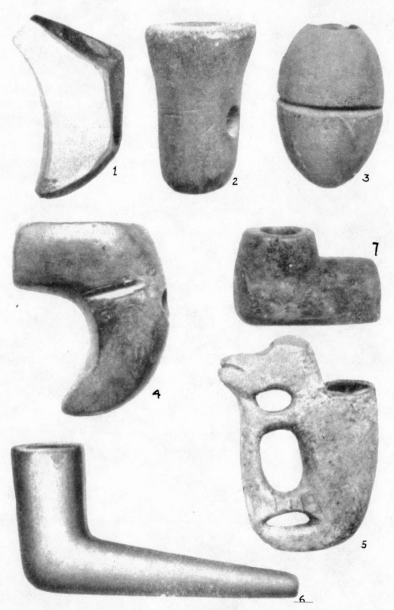

Plate 6. Erie Indian pipes, from Ripley, N. Y.

but through Iroquois eyes the French were doing more than fighting them.   They were espousing the cause of the Huron and joining with them as effective allies. Thereafter, the fate of France in the new world hung upon the outcome of the Huron-Iroquois war, though the French only . considered that it was a French-Iroquois war in which the Huron had been enlisted as aides, not realizing the nature of the contest.

The Iroquois as well as the Huron could win allies to their cause, and by rare fortune the Iroquois chose to court the enemies of France, the Dutch and the English. Thus, it was not long before the balance began to shift and Huron power commenced to wane,— and with it the hopes of New France. Of this we shall speak later, and show that with the breakup of the Huron tribes, after a frightfully bloody war, the Huron people were scattered like chaff, the Iroquois with their English allies rising as supreme dictators.

It may be asked why two races speaking the same general tongue did not unite in one great alliance, thus resisting European invasion and domination. We cannot always divine the direction that groups of men will take, or say why they act as they do, but we may venture to state that the Huron were jealous of the rising power of the confederated Iroquois, whom they considered a subordinate, defective and inferior people. The Huron were willing, however, to ally themselves with outer-nations, such as groups of the Algonkian, and use them in fighting their own kinsfolk. To the Iroquois this was a fatal and unforgivable transgression. The Iroquois urgently desired to promote a far-flung confederacy of all peoples who spoke the mother tongue, but to this the Huron and their allies, the Neutral, the Erie and Andaste (Conestoga), who spoke it, would not submit. Friction arose, and one act of aggression followed another. We shall not pursue the question further; all these people have gone, and with them the dreams of

France. Today, we speak English and the Iroquois are still with us. Their survival is mute testimony to the potency of a great ideal.

The defeated Huron became fugitives, their land was devastated, and refuge failed them. Stubborn pride had destroyed them, when surrender might have meant life and a new home, as it did to the Arendahronon villagers who yielded and were taken to the land of the Seneca and settled at Gandougarae, in Ontario county.*

The Huron were not the only members of the great Huron-Iroquoian family that looked upon the confederated Iroquois with bitter hatred. Another branch of that family in the Susquehanna valley feared and warred upon them as well. This was the Susquehannock-Andaste group of tribes, which, like the Huron, mustered Algonkian allies against the confederacy, and in the end failed.

10. The Andaste.

The Susquehannock and Conestoga dwelt along the Susquehanna river, and, if there were two separate divisions of this people, we should say that the Andaste or Conestoga dwelt in the upper valley and the Susquehannock in the lower, as far as the mouth of the river. Indeed, it was probably the lower river people that Captain John Smith met in 1608. The venturesome Captain was much impressed with their physical vigor and the style of their costumes, describing these and their weapons in detail in his quaint account, the History of Virginia.

The Conestoga or Andaste were enemies of the Seneca and their allies, and thus formed an important reserve for the Huron. In 1615, when the Huron persuaded Champlain to attack the Iroquois villages,

---

*This site is now found on the Marsh farm near East Bloomfield. Important as the site is, it has been "dug to death" and only an incomplete record made.

they relied upon the Andaste to come with a force of 500 warriors to assist in the investment. The Andaste were to march from the great town of Carantouan, possibly situated just below the present site of Waverly village, at the junction of the Chemung and Susquehanna. In anticipation of this, Champlain, with eight hundred Huron and Ottawa, reached the land of the Oneida, and began his attack. He struggled for several days, looked in vain for the arrival of the forces from Carantouan, and then fled in disorderly defeat, wounded and divested of all the glamour and awe with which he had formerly inspired his savage allies. After he had gone the Andaste did come, but too late to be of service. The victorious Oneida made the country unsafe for them and amid the derisive hoots of their enemies they retired as stealthily as they had come. Thus, did the millstones of the north and of the south fail to catch the Iroquois and grind them to extinction. The Iroquois were not without some apprehension in the matter, however, for they saw not only their league, but their very existence threatened on every side. Therefore, they forthwith resolved to have no enemies in the living world, and each Iroquois nation made the common resolve. This meant that every enemy should be destroyed. What followed is a most amazing story, and one without parallel.

11. Algonkian Enemies.

An account of the enemies of the Iroquois cannot be fairly concluded without some mention of the Algonkian tribes to the east and the south-east. These were the Mahican or Hudson river tribes, and the Delaware of eastern Pennsylvania and New Jersey. These feared and hated the confederated Iroquois, and with the New England Algonkian tribes and their allies and kinsfolk of the north—(the Ottawa, the Abenaki, and others to the further west), they made common cause against the people whom they called the Nation of Snakes—the Iroquois. The Mahican barred the Mohawk from the Hudson, and their Delaware allies controlled the upper reaches of the Susquehanna and Delaware.

Consider for a moment the Iroquois as they were situated. The Seneca of the Genesee country were faced by powerful enemies of their own bloodstock who were watchful of the Genesee frontier, and eager to make war. It took all the ingenuity of the Seneca to preserve peace and avoid complications. Indeed, they did endeavor to establish friendly relations with the Erie, the Neutral and the Huron, and for a time all was well, though bitter jealousy was plainly evident. On the south were the Andaste, on the east the Mahican, on the north, along the St. Lawrence, were the northern Huron and their allies. Here then was the Iroquois group of twenty thousand surrounded by a hostile group of a hundred thousand eager upon any pretext to launch an exterminating war. What gloomier outlook did any people ever face!

The confederated tribes of the Iroquois are so well known that no detailed description is here necessary, but for the sake of giving them a proper setting, and to establish their situation, let us review some of the salient features of this remarkable league.

12. The Five Brother Nations.*

It has been shown that all the Iroquoian tribes had a more or less independent position. The social organization of the stock, however, tended to induce closer unity of the larger branches, since by their clan system, all clansmen, of whatever tribe or nation, were called brothers. Thus, when the pressure of enemies made it necessary for brothers to unite to fight a common

---

*See the Constitution of the Five Nations, N. Y. State Museum Bulletin, 186, by A. C. Parker.

enemy, the idea of the confederation began to flourish. The nation itself was but the expansion of the clan, and the Confederacy of the nation. According to tradition it was Dekanawida, the Messiah of the North, who came bringing the proposition to unite Mohawk with their brother tribes, and later Hiawatha came from Onondaga with a similar plan in mind. In order to confirm their joint project, they secured the offices of Jikonsaseh, the Mother of Nations, the chieftainess of the Attiwendaronk, to accompany them in their tour in support of their scheme. An invitation was extended to all the nations to assemble about a symbolical "tree of peace". Though there was much adverse discussion, in the end only the Mohawk, the Oneida, the Onondaga, the Cayuga and the two divisions of the Seneca came. The tradition* is a lengthy, though interesting one, but the League was finally established, Adodarhoh, chief of the Onondaga, becoming its head.

Astonishing as it may seem, this league of the Five Nations, which might as well have been the league of many more nations, was dedicated to the purpose of establishing and enforcing universal peace. In the agreement which was drawn up the relations of the nations were carefully defined, and the laws of peace plainly set forth. The code of warfare was also laid down and proper pretexts of war agreed upon.

In this confederacy the Onondaga were to be the fire keepers, that is, they should preside over the council; the Mohawk should guard the east gate, and the Seneca should guard the west gate, provide the two war captains and control the entrance of other tribes from the west. The Cayuga and Oneida were to be "the younger brothers," who should care for captives.

Iroquois Government. Each nation of the League

---
*See the Constitution of the Five Nations, N. Y. State Museum Bulletin, 186, by A. C. Parker.

was to have its stated number of civil chiefs as members
of the League council, but, as the action of this council
had to be unanimous, the unequal distribution of civil
chiefs did not affect the rights of the nations in council.
For example, the Onondaga had fourteen representatives, while the two branches of the Seneca had only
eight. With all the nations these civil officers were
nominated by the women, and the councilmen only ratified the choice of the female nominators. Candidates
were chosen from groups of young men who had been
watched while in training, and who belonged to certain
hoyaneh or noble families. That any civil chief should
become a war captain or warrior while holding office as
a "Protector of the Great Peace," was forbidden.

The Confederacy, therefore, had a real government,
vested in a senate of fifty councilors, but it had no actual
President, this office being filled at each session by the
election of a moderator. The great Fire Keeper,
Adodarhoh, was only the nominal head for ceremonial
purposes, and he had no power to command or to
absolutely rule. All acts of the confederated council
were ratified by unanimous vote, brought by an ingenious method of voting by nations,—*en bloc*,—each
reporting to the Onondaga Fire Keepers the will of its
body. In the emergency of a tie the Onondaga Fire
Keepers had the casting vote, and following this all the
civil chiefs ratified the action, and thus the voice of the
Confederacy was singly for or against the measure
proposed.

This form of government theoretically meant
powerful support when war was declared or when it
became necessary to resist invasion. It seemed to say
that the armies of Five Nations would act as a unit. The
fear of this united action was especially dreaded by
enemies, who, taking advantage of the independent
rights of each constituent to make individual peace,

frequently sought to estrange the tribes one from the other in order to weaken the Confederacy. It is a well-known fact that the Seneca never had any great loyalty for the Mohawk, and that the Cayuga, the Onondaga and the Oneida, were a bit envious of the military strength of the Seneca and Mohawk. The astute leaders of the Confederacy were clever enough to use this seeming weakness to great advantage by allowing one of the nations to make peace with the enemy, and then inviting its warriors to enlist under the leadership of one of the warring nations, which left a pledged place of refuge when fighting became too warm for them. Thus, a seeming weakness, infringed upon, proved in reality to be a point of strength.

The Iroquois Peace Policy. It seems a contradiction to state that Iroquois government was founded upon the desire to establish universal peace. Nevertheless, they did desire to establish a firm peace, but, as brave and adventurous men, they were jealous of their honor and not afraid to fight. As the Iroquois government was one of social pressure, resting upon the opinions of the populace, rather than upon the will of over-lords, the young men frequently seized upon a popular complaint as a pretext for war, and, though their nation had not officially declared war, they embarked on expeditions against hereditary enemies. For these untoward acts the whole nation sometimes received punishment, and most of the smaller Iroquois wars resulted from such unauthorized raids.

There is something within civilized as well as savage men that makes warfare an inviting pursuit, and these Indians simply followed the common human urge to fight and kill members of the outer groups. The lure of war springs from something more primitive than reason; it is a primordial form of race "cannibalism," whereby one group devours another.

In the manner described lived the Five Nations, stretching through the heart of the Empire State, from the mouth of the Schoharie, along the Mohawk, through the region of the Finger Lakes, to the valley of the pleasant Genesee.   Each nation had its own domain with well-known boundaries, each had its villages and principal town, and each had its own hunting range.

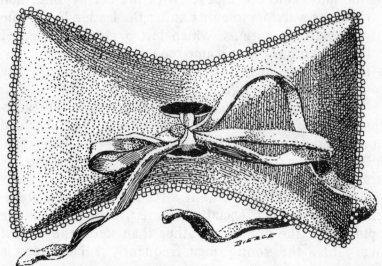

Fig. 2. Hair ornament resembling a stone "gorget". It is of skin stretched over a wooden frame.

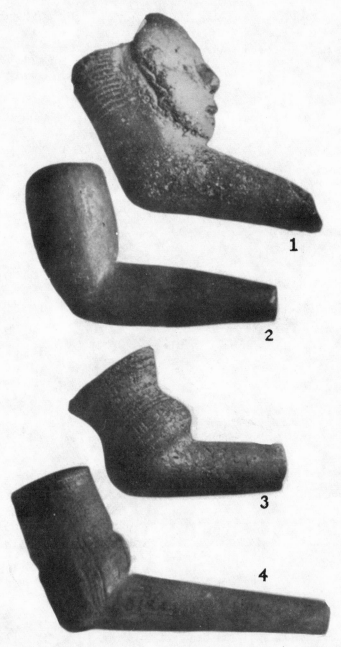

Plate 7. Algonkian pipes of the fourth period, from Finger Lakes region.

II. THE SENECA.

The Seneca, as "Keepers of the Western Door," had at their eastern boundary the western slopes of the hills east of Seneca Lake, taking in most of Schuyler county, and skimming the northern boundaries of Tioga and Chemung, though later, as they overcame their enemies, they dropped their line far down into Pennsylvania. The early Seneca country occupied only the highlands of southern and western Ontario county, for the Seneca came from some locality west of the Genesee, perhaps by way of the Alleghany and thence through the Dansville district.   Gradually, they spread to the north and to the east, taking in Canandaigua, Keuka, and Seneca lakes.   Expansion westward gave them possession of Honeoye, Canadice, Hemlock and Conesus lakes, and when the white man took possession their towns flourished along the Genesee.   Then they were open villages with no stockades to protect them, for by that time the Seneca had slain or adopted their foes, and the might of Seneca arms was a powerful enough barrier to keep the enemy at a respectful distance from their settlements.

The Name of the Seneca. The Seneca are the "People of the Hill".   Both history and tradition assert this, and the Seneca people who faithfully remember their tradition speak of themselves even yet in connection with a certain great hill in the land of their ancestors.   It is possible that this may have been Bare Hill on the east shore of Canandaigua lake, but, though many authorities have asserted that this is the spot, it is yet by no means certain that the hill of their tradition is not the great South Hill that skirts the lake from the Vine Valley to the marsh lands that border the inlet at Woodville.   Students who have gone over the region in detail and who have examined the ground feel that

Bare Hill is not *the* hill of the Seneca tradition, but an ingenious substitute. Even so, the Seneca are still the "people of the hill," for their designation is Djiionondo-wanen-aka. In every tongue of the aborigines about them they were called so, and Cartier, the first explorer (1534-35) who saw the Iroquois, heard of them under the name Trudamini. Champlain knew of them as Entouhonorons and Chouontouarouon (Chonontoua-ronon), and the earliest of the Jesuits recorded the name as Tsonontouan and Sonontouan, leaving off the *ronon* meaning "people" or "tribe".

The name *Seneca*, as we know it today, is of Algonkian origin, coming from O-sin-in-ka, meaning "People of the Stone". The Dutch called all the tribes west of the Mohawk "Sinnekars," but as each tribe in turn denied this name and pointed further west, it came to be applied to the Nunda-waga (Sonontouan), and the name was still further corrupted to "Seneca," thus confusing a Roman surname with an Algonkian term.

1.   The Situation of the Seneca People.

The Ganarqua-Canandaigua group had its chief town on what is now called Boughton Hill, a mile south of the present village of Victor, Ontario county. Here, it seems to have been established as early as 1650, probably having moved from some more southerly locality either in the East Bloomfield or Bristol region. The Boughton Hill village had the Seneca name of Ga-o-sa-eh-ga-aah, but the French, taking the Mohawk word, called it Gannagaro, which has survived in local history. The name means, "There the basswood bark lies," referring to the bark conductor through which flowed the water from the spring. At least this is the conclusion of O. H. Marshall, who cites John Blacksmith, an aged Tonawanda chief, as his informant. The name may have had a deeper meaning, however, for Gannagaro was established as the principal town of the eastern division of the Seneca people. In the symbolism of the Iroquois the western door of the Confederacy was "guarded by sheets of slippery bark upon which the enemy would slip if he sought unwarranted and uninvited admittance". Far and wide among the Iroquois Gannagaro was known as the metropolis of the Seneca people, and many distinguished visitors came to it. When the French missionaries erected their chapel there they gave the mission and the village the name of St. James.

About three miles south of Gannagaro was the village of Gandougarae, as the French spelled it, though the Seneca sometimes called it Chi-nos-hah-geh.* It was a village in which Huron, Neutral, Erie and other captives were held pending their "senecazation," the acculturation of aliens being a part of a scheme that kept the Iroquois numerically powerful, since by it they repaired their military losses.

In this aboriginal paradise, teeming with game, fish and birds, lived the Seneca people, secure in the feeling that their abundant fields of produce, together with the natural supplies of wild foods and forest beasts, would give sustenance and safety. Indeed, after they had driven out the earlier Algonkian occupants they lived in comparative security.

Unauthorized Raids. Though their civil customs were based upon principles of peace and though their civil chiefs were pledged to strive for peace and its preservation, the raids of their northern enemies kept in mind their old-time grievances, and it is to be believed that unauthorized parties of young Seneca braves frequently stirred up trouble that might have been ordinarily avoided. In the minds of the young men the instinctive love of war was ever present, and

---

*Vide, Marshall's Writings, p. 139. The actual origin of Gannagaro, however, is in the Seneca word Ga-nan-no-ga'-eh, "Hickory-bark-lies-up".

no amount of reasoning by their elders could eradicate the desire to seek out and slay their enemies. War was in the blood itself; it was a trait that the "Great Binding Law of Peace" could not easily blot out. Thus, adventurous young warriors announced themselves war chiefs and organized expeditions against their hereditary enemies. This resulted in reprisals and soon the whole league found itself involved in wars with many tribes and bands. It must not be believed, however, that all these wars were brought upon them by their own desires, for certain enemies, as the Huron, had long assailed them and sought their ruin. It will be recalled that when Champlain first heard of the Iroquois he knew of them as the race against which his Huron friends fought. Thus, the great events of Iroquois history cluster about the episodes of the Huron-Iroquois war, a war in which the French espoused the cause of the Hurons, and later the English that of the Iroquois. This war the Senecas probably did not start, it being very likely a feud in the beginning between the Mohawk and lower Huron, but for many years the Seneca bore the brunt of the fray and in the end they finished it and absorbed the Huron or guarded them in sequestered places, to the peril of their other divisions, for the Huron descendants inherited a love for the French.

2. The War with the French.

The French, naturally sympathetic with the convert Huron, among whom they dwelt, kept up a desultory war against the Iroquois, killing them wherever they found them, but in 1633 the Iroquois turned the tables and began to seriously harass the French, even boarding a shallop. The next year the Seneca sent out an expedition against the Huron and defeated them so decisively that the Huron confederacy made overtures for peace. This was welcomed officially by the Iroquois, who really desired to unite all the nations of the mother tongue, providing these would acknowledge the supremacy of the "Great Binding Law of Peace" and become constituent nations of the Iroquois confederacy. This was one of the aims of the Iroquois war, though it was complicated by revenge and by raids of young warriors who merely wanted adventure where legitimate prey could be found.

Reprisals. Peace negotiations were in process during 1635 and the Seneca declared a truce. A young Seneca warrior, however, being dissatisfied went to the Onondaga where he married a young woman of that nation. Here he argued against the Huron and sought opportunity to take the field against them. Upon a certain occasion he was fishing in Lake Ontario, when he was captured by a Huron party and finally tortured and killed. During the same year certain Huron and Algonkian allies burned some Iroquois prisoners and raided an Iroquois camp. The Iroquois were now inflamed not only against the Huron but against the French who upheld them. In reprisal they attacked a Huron party on Lake St. Peter, capturing thirty prisoners (1637). At the same time they sent one hundred and fifty warriors to a nearby French settlement and set up the symbol of their presence, a series of sticks attached to a tree. It was a bold challenge.

The older and wiser councillors of the Huron urged their tribesmen to seek a permanent peace, for during this year the Wenroh-ronon (separated people), had sought refuge with them and spread tales of Seneca power. The response to this advice was a raid by young Huron, who marched against the Seneca, which so involved their nation that support was necessary. Two years later (1639), the Huron defeated an Oneida war party led by Oronkouaia. They captured the chief and

tortured him horribly. The account of this affair is one
of the most horrible in all the annals of Indian warfare,
but we are told that the Oneida withstood the torture to
the end, defying his captors by song and invective to
make any torture hard enough to cause an Iroquois to
cry out in pain.

The Oneida was soon revenged, for the Iroquois by
quick, bold moves, struck here and there with amazing
rapidity, coming and going almost unseen, destroying
remote Algonkian villages and wiping out one entire
Huron town, sparing few and torturing hundreds of
luckless captives.

Iroquois Success. Their small companies, quickly
handled, were everywhere, and by 1653 the French
began to realize that the situation was desperate, for
now the Seneca and their allies had guns which they
handled all too well. Even French prisoners were not
now respected, and Father Jouges and his colleagues
were frightfully tortured, and his friend Goupil was
killed in one of the Mohawk towns (1642). So successful were the Iroquois that it became unsafe for any
Frenchman to wander far into the woods or to build his
cabin far from a fort. As for the Indians, small settlements were soon wiped out and the smaller villages fled
to the larger Huron towns for refuge. Occasionally the
Huron or Algonkian allies had some spectacular success.
One Huron even penetrated the forest and entered the
Seneca capital on Boughton Hill, cutting his way into
a bark cabin and taking several scalps, but this availed
but little, and war continued, its harrowing details being
recorded day by day by the Jesuit fathers, who were
powerless to mitigate the evils they saw.

The Huron Sue for Peace. The beginning of the
end was in sight in 1647 when the Huron sent deputies
to the Andaste on the Susquehanna, pleading for
assistance to the dying "mother nation". The distress

of the Huron even impressed the Onondaga who were
disposed to grant peace, and who sent Civil Chief Skandawati* with an escort and fifteen Huron prisoners to
the Huron council, to discuss a permanent truce. The
Seneca and Mohawk, however, objected to any peace
proposals that did not mean complete surrender. Still
the Huròn, hoping for peace, sent an embassy to the
Onondaga, but it was treacherously attacked and some
of the ambassadors killed. When Skandawati heard of
this his heart was broken, for he had pledged his honor,
—and his kinsfolk had counted it as naught. He brooded
over this affront and shortly after sought out a secluded
place and plunged a knife into his own heart. Warrior
though he was, after the fashion of the day, he would
not countenance treachery, nor could he endure life
when honor had been stained by the over-acts of folly.

In 1648 the Seneca defeated a Huron hunting party
with which was an Onondaga hostage in charge of a
captive, but instead of accepting his release, he demanded a safe conduct with his charge, for, being an
ambassador of peace he said that he would sooner "die
than . . . to appear to have acted as their enemy".
He was allowed to go his way, for such in those days was
honor esteemed among savages.

3. The Fall of Huronia.

In July, 1648, the Huron town of Teanaustate (the
mission of St. Joseph) was attacked, together with a
nearby settlement and in all 700 captives were taken by
the Iroquois. The records show that more than 400
families were destroyed, scattered or captured, and the
mission of Father Antonine Daniel laid in ruins. The

*Beyond the Rapids, a sachem war captain. This name is also
spelled Skunniwundi. It is one of the most famous names in the
legendary lore of all the Huron-Iroquois people. The present writer has
employed it in his "Skunny Wundy Stories," for young people,—Doran,
1926.

Iroquois had not even yet spent their fury and had other cunning plans. During that autumn they collected an army of 1,000 men, who, taking their ease, hunted their way to the Huron domain, breasting the winter's cold and hardening themselves by the strenuous demands of forest life. On the 15th of March, 1648 they adroitly encompassed the stockaded walls of Taenhatentaron, the mission of St. Ignace, and began a survey of its strong palisades and moat. A weak spot was found and enlarged. Like wraiths the Iroquois warriors penetrated the town and began the attack. The battle raged; ten Iroquois were killed, four hundred Hurons fell, and only three escaped. It was like the Iroquois to strike such blows, swift, certain and conclusive.

Fate of the Huron. At sunrise the Iroquois marched a league onward to the fortified mission of St. Louis, invested it and quickly overcame the eighty warriors who remained to defend it, for all others had fled with the harrowing news that the Iroquois were coming. Victorious, the Iroquois then returned to St. Ignace to refresh themselves before attacking the Catholic mission station, but found it too well defended for a fight that would not cost them many lives. By the next morning three hundred Huron had rallied and begun counter attack, but they had lost heart and with it the effective-ness of their warriors; they fled as night came on— scattering like the leaves where they might.

The conquerors remained to torture the priests, who were compelled to witness hideous atrocities, many of which were not unlike the horrors of the Christian Inquisition in Europe.

Huronia was terrorized, and five of the principal towns were completely abandoned, the people fleeing to any available retreat in search of refuge. The great town of Scanenaenrat unconditionally surrendered and requested to be united with their conquerors that the

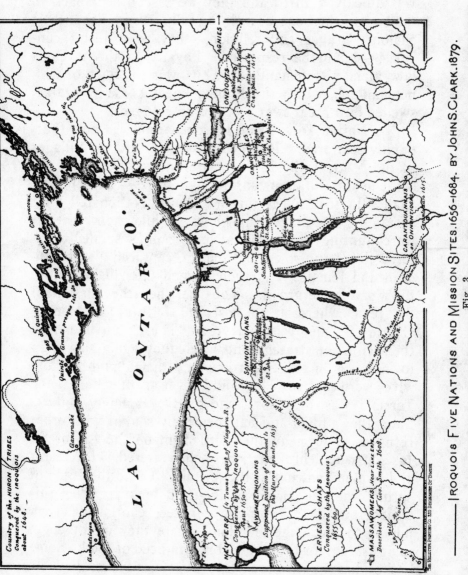

IROQUOIS FIVE NATIONS AND MISSION SITES. 1656-1684. BY JOHN S. CLARK. 1879.
Fig. 3.

people might indeed become Seneca. Their petition was quickly granted and they were soon sent back to the land of the Seneca, with the full assurance that their customs, usages and religion,—they were Jesuit converts,—should be respected. Loyalty to the Iroquois laws alone was demanded. Thus, was the town of Chinos-hah-geh, which the French knew as Gandougarae, swelled by a great swarm of Huron refugees.

A Nation Dies. The Huron nation was now thoroughly scattered. Refugees swarmed into the villages of the Neutral, the Erie, the Petun, and even into the settlements of far distant foreign tribes,—but of little avail. In 1649 the Petun or Tobacco Nation fell after sustaining one staggering blow. While their warriors were hunting the Iroquois, the Iroquois suddenly entered the Petun town of Etharita, captured all its children and females, and then burned the village before the warriors returned. Thus perished the mission of St. Jean, where at his post the faithful missionary Charles Garnier was martyred. The Petun had been the victims of strategy and when they again saw their town it was in smoking ruins, and their daughters and wives were captives who would never again behold them. Terrible was the blow, and grief was agony indeed. Later they rallied and half heartedly sought with other refugees to form another settlement on the isle of St. Joseph, where broken tribesmen wintered, with terror and famine gnawing at their vitals. Came the signs of spring when the ice was about to break. Over this treacherous floor groups of refugees cautiously crept, hoping to reach the mainland where they might begin their fishing, for they were sorely in need of food. Some broke through the ice, but the majority reached the shore where they divided into small parties. All seemed well, but they might have suspected that the unforgiving Iroquois would seek them out; still hunger was a stern master and forced them to search for sustenance. Could they have only known that their conquerors had an ambush well prepared for them! Such was the case, and all but one were killed. "My pen," wrote Ragueneau, "has no ink black enough to describe the fury of the Iroquois."

Refugees. Under Jesuit leadership an expedition was formed to take the melancholy survivors to Quebec, where they might have the protection of the French garrisons. Cautiously, the party proceeded in canoes, finding on their way, both the mournful ashes of their own villages and towns and the remains of the fortified camps of the conquering Five Nations' war parties. Huronia was abandoned, and by 1650 not a town or mission remained. Scores of refugees sought asylums, some among the Algonkian tribes and some with the Andaste kinsfolk on the Susquehanna. Outcasts of two large Huron villages petitioned the Seneca for peace and adoption, and found their prayer immediately granted upon the usual voluntary obligation on the part of the petitioners to become loyal Seneca subjects. The unreconciled found homes at Loretto, nine miles from Quebec, and today in the village of New Loretto their descendants may be seen, but they have totally forgotten their own language and speak only French patois.

The mighty Huron nation, far outnumbering the Iroquois, passed as a power, though small bands from time to time sought revenge, only to be punished by another frightful Iroquois blow that again sapped their numbers. With the Huron out of the way, the French now received the military attention of the Iroquois, and no French settlement or fortification was safe from attack.

4. Destruction of the Neutral and Erie.

The Neutral War. During the Huron war the Neutral Nation or Attiwendaronk had kept an honest peace, and this amid great perplexities and temptation, for the Huron were closely akin to them and better loved than Iroquois. To their credit, however, they offered no military assistance one way or the other, save by extending the customary refuge to the homeless Huron. The Iroquois now began to cast suspicious eyes at the overflowing Attiwendaronk towns, looking for signs of Huron recuperation. A pretext presented itself, and in 1650 the Neutral were accused of a breach of faith upon grounds that appear rather untenable when related by their Jesuit proponents. Apparently, the Iroquois saw trouble growing and sought to nip it in the bud. Thus, in the autumn of 1650, the Iroquois by a swift and terrible attack reduced one of the frontier towns of the Neutral garrisoned by 1,600 warriors. The warriors were routed and young people led away into captivity. The next spring another town was attacked with the same results, and soon every Neutral town was ravished and the populace scattered. Hundreds and perhaps thousands were made captives and settled among the Iroquois, to forget their national origin and to become Iroquois.

It was in this war that Jikonsaseh, the traditional Mother of Nations, was taken captive and carried away to the settlment on the Ganarqua (Mud Creek in East Bloomfield, Ontario county). Thus, tradition tells us that the Seneca became the guardians of the descendant of "the first woman born on earth," the arbiter of peace.

Algonkian Raids. For two years the Seneca and their allies kept up their raids against the French and their Algonkian hoardes, in general meeting success, though their reverses at times were stunning. In 1653 they offered peace to the French and consummated a treaty, to the great relief of New France and her Indian partisans. The Mohawk now hunted and roamed in fraternal accord with the Algonkian bands, learning everything that they could as to conditions, policy and military strength.   It was a shrewd move on the part of the sagacious Iroquois, for another contest was to be waged in another field and Frenchmen were not wanted as enemies.

Rumors of this new venture of the Iroquois, whom one might believe were weary of war, came in various ways.   An Onondaga sachem at Montreal in an address related that his people were now to fall upon the Erie and destroy them; and the Erie were the last of formidable enemies in the north.   They lay west of the Genesee from the mouth of the Cattaraugus westward along Lake Erie and southward beyond the Alleghany.   They had numerous towns and villages and a population of more than 14,000, if early estimates are to be accepted.   This meant that they had between 2,500 and 4,000 war-riors who must be overcome.

The Erie War.   The Erie had many matters to discuss with their Seneca neighbors, and in the year 1653 (circa) they sent thirty ambassadors to the Seneca town of Sonnontouan* to hold a conference.   During this meeting a member of the Erie party murdered a Seneca.   As this act occurred during an inter-tribal peace council, it was construed by the haughty Seneca as an unpardonable insult, and twenty-five Erie ambas-sadors were slain, five escaping to return with the tragic story.

War was now inescapable, and though the Seneca and their allies were powerful, the Erie were an even match for them, especially as they had with them several thousand Huron refugees eagerly awaiting an oppor-tunity to enter a successful contest.

Annenraes.   The Erie struck the first blow, cutting

---

*The site of this famous town is at the bend of the Honeoye near Rochester Junction, Monroe county.   It is otherwise called Totiakton.

off the rear guard of a returning Seneca expedition, and killing its eighty picked men, later assailing a Seneca town and burning it.   Erie scouts with great bravery appeared at the very gates of another village and captured Annenraes, one of the most respected and loved of the Onondaga chiefs.   It was he who had been captured by the Huron in 1647, condemned to death and tactfully allowed to escape by the Huron chiefs.   Crossing Lake Ontario by canoe, he found eight hundred Seneca and Cayuga, headed by a band of three hundred Onondaga, ready to make a quick crossing and to revenge his death.   His home-coming was like a resurrection miracle, and there was great rejoicing.   Now that the Erie had carried him away, the rage of the Iroquois was kindled anew, especially as Annenraes did not know that war had been declared.

The old chief was taken to an Erie town, and in the absence of an old woman who had lost her son, was assigned to her, in the fond hope that she would kindly receive him as a substitute, and that he would then act as a peace-maker.   When the matron returned, however, she was angered at the plan of adopting a chief of her enemies and ordered that he be submitted to the customary torture.   According to traditions this was her undeniable privilege, and all the arguments of the Erie chiefs could not move her from the vicarious demand.   Annenraes was torn from the feast of adoption, stripped of his robes and ignominiously burned at the stake, crying out as the flames gnawed their way into his flesh, that by this act the Erie were burning their own nation, for his people would mete out a complete revenge.   His words were fulfilled to the letter.

The Iroquois Strike. Upon the heels of this tragedy, 1,800 Iroquois warriors fully equipped were soon under way in their war canoes.   Landing in the Erie domain, they carried their canoes with them, for

Erie land was one of streams. Soon the great town of Rique was reached, but where this was situated it is not easy to state, though from archeological evidence it may have been in the lower Cattaraugus valley and have been the eastmost Erie settlement. From Jesuit *Relations* we learn the details of the assault. Two Iroquois war captains were dressed in French military uniforms, and marching their warriors to the Erie stockade, demanded an unconditional surrender. One of the chiefs even in gentle tones urged a capitulation, indicating thereby that peace was preferable to war, and urged the Erie to yield that they might live. "The Master of Life fights for us," the chief called out to the Erie. "You will be ruined if you resist him!"

"Who is this Master of Life?" sneered the Erie leader. "We acknowledge none but our arms and hatchets." Upon this retort the Iroquois, who had surrounded the fort, rushed upon it, with their canoes as shields, using them as scaling ladders. The Erie fought desperately, showering the air with poisoned arrows, but at last their walls were broken and the Onondaga, as the nation seeking first revenge, entered the town where they overcame their foes in so terrible a carnage that the ground was knee deep in blood. A reinforcement of 300 Erie appeared at daybreak and made the gestures of combat, but fell back in dismay as the Iroquois arose to their feet with terrifying war cries.

The Erie Exterminated. In one fell stroke the Erie nation had passed on, but so terrible were the losses of the Iroquois that they spent the remainder of the season nursing their wounded and burying their dead. Many Erie refugees voluntarily surrendered and yielded allegiance to the confederacy, and the 600 who sought protection were given full immunity. The Erie nation was not only to be a memory, but there is little doubt that under the name of Mingo many wandered into Ohio and even sought refuge among the Cherokee. The Iroquois even allowed the captives who had voluntarily surrendered and plighted their word to remain in little towns along the Cattaraugus, and archeological research has proven that there was a continuous occupation of this valley from this time, 1654-56, on until this very day.   The old Seneca town of Cattaraugus may have had as its original nucleus these defeated Erie people, and many of the Ohio Seneca settlements may have been naturalized Erie captives.

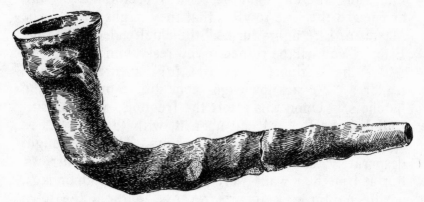

Fig. 4.   Seneca pipe of about 1650.

5.   The Seneca War upon New France.

After the Erie war, the Iroquois began to harass the French settlements and to raid the refugee Huron and their Algonkian friends.   This brought on new complications between the Seneca and Mohawk, who for a while were at the point of war, but at a general council held at Onondaga, July 24, 1656, the differences were smoothed by arbitration.   After this the Mohawk, never over friendly with their allies, feared reprisals and asked the Dutch for protection should they be attacked by the Seneca, for they had trouble enough with the Andaste to the south.   They did not want another menace.

Plate 8. King Hendrick (Soi-en-ga-rah-ta). Sachem of the Mohawk Nation, son of a Mahikan father and a Mohawk mother, Colonel in the British colonial forces and stalwart friend of English civilization. Hendrick was born 1680 (circa) and lost his life in the Battle of Lake George under Johnson in 1755. One of his most celebrated orations was delivered at the Albany Conference in Albany, 1754. Painting by Wm. A. McKenna, owned by Frank L. Reuss and reproduced by his permission.

The French Seek an Iroquois Alliance. As a precaution the French found it policy to woo the friendship of the Iroquois nations through the kind ministrations of the Catholic missionaries, but it was a case where politics and religion were badly mixed. The priests won many converts and made hosts of friends, and this the French colonial officials were willing to capitalize for military and political advantage, to the injury of the missionary fathers and the cause of Christianity. The Iroquois were at first pleased with the priests, but later began to see them in the guise of unwitting agents of New France. With this suspicion, all pretexts of peace were abandoned and war against Canada was resumed.

The Seneca kept up their forays for ten years after the Erie war, and were ceaseless in their onslaughts upon French settlements. They also sent war parties elsewhere, as against the Minisink and the Andaste, at this time generally called the Minqua. Events now followed with amazing rapidity, and so fickle were the kaleidoscopic changes and readjustments that it is only with confusion that even a critical scholar can follow the treaties, the councils, the raids, the complications and ramifications of Iroquois warfare.

6. The Andaste War.

The Seneca were determined among other things to end the existence of the Andaste (Conastoga, Minqua). The Andaste had been stormed by the Cayuga, the Mohawk, the Oneida and the Onondaga, but could not be defeated. They somehow always managed to inflict a blow in retaliation for attacks. The Mohawk between 1650 and 1660 had fared badly in their Andaste war, and now the Seneca resolved to have a decisive battle, or to seal a lasting peace,—which, the Andaste should say by words or weapons.

An Iroquois war party had hovered about the great Andaste capital on the Susquehanna, and the twenty-five warriors who had entered with proposals of peace, though some authorities state that their mission was one of treachery,—were burned on scaffolds that rose high above the palisades, permitting their friends to witness their punishment. This brought on a ten years' war, lasting until in 1672, when a party of sixty Seneca and Cayuga were attacked by sixty young Andaste and put to flight with losses. There was never any doubt as to Andaste bravery and daring. For three years more the Seneca fought them, until, finally in 1675, the last of the great enemies of the Iroquois were subdued. The survivors found refuge in the various Iroquois towns, particularly the Oneida, but many were colonized in little settlements on the Susquehanna where they were known as Connestoga. Those who wandered afar mingled with refugee Erie and bands of wandering Seneca and Cayuga who were afield,—and became the Mingo of later history.

7. Dilution of Iroquois Blood.

All these wars, lasting as they did from 1630 to 1675, had reduced the Iroquois by nearly one-half, and yet by their policy of adoption and naturalization, they had an even greater population in their towns than when they began their bloody onslaughts. The captives whom they adopted were generally well treated, once they had proved beyond peradventure that they were utterly loyal,—but if there was any suspicion they were sometimes mistreated, and even killed at the whim of their sponsors. So far as Iroquoian blood was concerned it still predominated, for the Confederated Iroquois chose the best of their own linguistic stock. It must be noted, however, that *the power that lay behind the Iroquois was not the tribal government as such, but the dynamic ideals and moral force of its social organization.*

Thus, it was that we have evidence in the *Relation of* 1660, that the Seneca were made up of eleven refugee nations and the Onondaga of seven. Captives were not asked to fight against their own people, but were expected to volunteer on war parties against any other nation. During the period of their first adoption they did not enter into the discussions of the councils, but as they proved their integrity some were even made chiefs and their children were regarded as Iroquois, to the manor born.

8. War with the Illinois.

Southern Raids. With the defeat of the Andaste the Iroquois, especially the Seneca, began to push their way southward, down the Susquehanna, in search of their enemies. This caused the settlers in Maryland much anxiety. It seemed as if the Seneca were everywhere, for distance and enemy barriers made little difference. We hear of them at Quebec and Montreal, planning raids on the Mississippi and spreading terror through Maryland, though when Governor Andros sought an adjustment, an amicable arrangement was made at a treaty in Albany.

War with the Illinois. During the year 1680, the Seneca determined to exterminate the Illinois, and by playing upon the jealousy of the Miamis, induced them to join them in an expedition. The French explorer, LaSalle, was now in the land of the Illinois, for these people were allies of the French, and the source of a valuable peltry market. Tonti, "of the Iron hand," his faithful retainer, had become separated from him, causing LaSalle much anxiety, but Tonti was safe enough in the great town of the Illinois and here witnessed the coming of the Seneca and saw their initial attack. He did what he could to bring about peace and to protect his allies, but was wounded in the attempt by the Seneca who as a Frenchman distrusted him. An Onondaga interposed on his behalf, for trouble was not wanted just now with the French, to whom they had promised peace. Tonti was compelled to listen to the harrangue of the Iroquois war chiefs, who ordered him to return home, promising that they would "not eat the Illinois". Tonti, with great reluctance, departed in a leaky canoe in which were two friars,—Membre and Robourde. He had seen the Illinois abandon and burn their great village and flee down the river and had seen Iroquois taking possession of it and building a stockade. It was enough.

Deprived of their victims, the Iroquois lashed themselves into a frenzy and tore into splinters the grave houses of the Illinois dead, mutilating such of the corpses as they could find, and in derision taking the skulls as decorations for their stockade, that the Illinois might be infuriated still more. Then they pursued the Illinois down the river, following on the opposite bank, camping each night face to face with their terrified foes. The Illinois fled to the mouth of the Illinois river and here divided their bands, some ascending the Mississippi and others pushing westward, hoping that, after all, the Seneca and their allies did not actually wish to destroy them, but merely drive them out of their homeland. One tribe, the Tamaroas, foolishly decided to remain at the mouth of their river, and being attacked, quickly fled, leaving their women and children as victims to the rage of their enemies. Many were tortured and slain and hundreds were made captive and taken back to Iroquoia. The story of this terrible contest is vividly told by Parkman in *LaSalle and the Discovery of the Great West*. Indeed, it was Parkman who located the site of the Illinois town at Starved Rock and discovered many relics of that occupation. The Illinois were thoroughly defeated but not exterminated, and later returned to their ancient seats under the protection of the French, who built forts in strategic places among them. Nevertheless, the Seneca determined that war against the Illinois should go on, and forty-three chiefs at Montreal in August, 1683, stood by while the Seneca delegates frankly proclaimed that "the Illinois must die".

9. The Punitive Expeditions of France.

LaBarre's Expedition. De la Barre, the French commander, now resolved to prepare to punish this insolence and the next year he seized a Seneca ambassador and his escort on the ground that the Seneca had seized a French boat full of goods. He then made elaborate preparations to equip an expedition to subdue that haughty nation. With his boats and nine hundred men he proceeded, landing at LaFamine on the Salmon river at its juncture with Lake Ontario. Here, many of his men fell sick with fever. A few Onondaga came to greet him, and their welcome was so characterized by sarcasm and mockery that De la Barre was furious when he understood its import. It was a stream of caustic eloquence that is scarcely equaled anywhere in the history of oratory. If the French came for peace Garangula (Hotreauate), the orator, asked, why they should have come with so many warriors and weapons? The sophisticated Iroquois knew what all this preparation really meant and, continued the orator, "our children and old men had carried their bows and arrows into the heart of your camp, if our warriors had not disarmed them and kept them back". Then, referring to their onslaughts against the Indian allies of the French, Garangula explained that his people had merely captured a band that was carrying arms to use against them, and reminded the French that this was a legitimate precaution. He boldly proclaimed that the

Iroquois would not be ordered by anyone to trade with any nation, but would make its own choice.

The enraged De la Barre, after this browbeating by an old Iroquois, knew that further deceit was impossible, and that he must return to Canada without doing anything other than revealing his distressed condition. It was with great relish, therefore, that he responded to the order of Louis XIV to capture Iroquois prisoners and return them to France as slaves for the royal galleys, as though Spanish experience in the Indies had not shown that the natives of America made poor slaves.

10. The Coming of Denonville.

The pressure brought to bear by the Iroquois now caused New France to abandon her Illinois allies, which was most displeasing to Louis. The desire of France was to have an open road up the Mississippi and Ohio, in order to effect a juncture with the Canadian colonies. This hold would have permitted a continental penetration, and to insure this the Illinois were needed as an offset to the Seneca and their allies. A stronger hand was plainly needed, and De la Barre was recalled to France and the Marquis Denonville sent to assume the governorship of New France and to command her military forces (1685). Denonville had royal orders to assist the Illinois and to humble the Iroquois. He quickly established himself, securing the respect of the *habitans*, the soldiers and the native red men.

Denonville's Expedition. Denonville soon gaged his material, and then began to carry out the plan of his ruler. He mustered his troops in May, 1687, and took them to Quebec, where he began to build his batteaux. By June 13th his army was ready for its expedition of conquest. His forces consisted of one thousand, six hundred seasoned continental soldiers, nine hundred and eighty-three Indians and four hundred *habitans*. Such was the army which set forth from Montreal and landed at Irondequoit bay on July 10, 1687.

To protect the supplies a fort was constructed, consuming two days' effort, and a guard of four hundred and forty men was left in charge of boats and provisions. Three days after landing, the party with forces of Ottawa allies began the march toward the Seneca town of Gannagaro. Three defiles were passed, and an attack made at the third by a force of Seneca. These were repulsed and on July 14th the French expedition was held on the battlefield until noon, when it advanced, crossed the lowlands and ascended the hill to the Seneca village, which they found burning and deserted. Here, they encamped, sheltering themselves as best they could from the heavy rain storm. Their work of destruction had been done for them by the dismayed Seneca, and before the French lay the charred and blackened village of Gannagaro, the greatest settlement of the Seneca people. Most of its one hundred and thirty lodges were charred wrecks. The inhabitants had escaped into the forest to the east, seeking shelter in smaller hamlets, some went to the Cayuga, far across the hills and swamps. Many of the warriors fled to the stockaded hill a mile and a half across the valley to the west, but the next day upon attack they fled in terror. Denonville's savages hunted down the old, the decrepid, and the wounded, killing and scalping without stint. It was as if all the enemies of the Seneca had come at once to witness their humiliation. Even seven Illinois appeared upon the scene stripped bare and ready for revenge. The French militia spent its time cutting down cornfields and breaking open corn cribs and public granaries. They determined that no food be left should the Seneca survive and return to Gannagaro, but that the land of the foe should be desolate. indeed.

Each of the four great villages was visited, and each pillaged and burned, all valuables and food being destroyed.   Denonville in his journal describes the immense quantity of corn, estimating that 1,200,000 bushels, new and old, were destroyed by fire, but he probably was guilty of Gallic exaggeration, or relied upon false reports.

Results of the Raid. With Denonville were a number of Mohawk Indians, among them the great chief. Kyrn, and the grandfather of Chief Brant. These were not averse to killing their Seneca kinsfolk, for whom they never had great love.   When all was done, the French and their red allies did not achieve their end, for the Seneca were not destroyed, as had been hoped. This the allies who came with the French were quick to perceive, for they had been cheated of their bloody ambition to kill every Seneca in the land of Sonnontouan.   It was with a feeling of disgust that they returned to their base on the bay of Irondequoit, for they were jeering the French as "corn cutters" instead of slayers of men.   Nevertheless, the red allies of France bore away with them a goodly number of scalps. and there were few whose blades were not red with gore. The Seneca suffered, it is true, and their season's supply of corn was gone, yet, like hornets whose nest had been crushed, they were humming in the woods and burning with revenge.   They now determined that the French should feel their sting. New France in time knew that the Seneca could remember and strike back with vigor. Invasion had but lighted a conflagration which could not be extinguished.   Another war was on!

Denonville, in returning, took his troops from Irondequoit to Niagara, where he built a fort which he garrisoned with one hundred men, in order that the country might be held in the name of France.   He then

Plate 9. Sir William Johnson. Superintendent for the British Crown of the Indians of North America, particularly the Six Nations. This picture is reproduced from the collection of historical water colors owned by Frank L. Reuss.

returned to Quebec, following the north shore of
Lake Ontario.

The Seneca Seek England's Protection. When the
Seneca, filled with revenge, returned to their settlements, they found them in a welter of blood and ashes.
Gannagaro, Gannondata, Gandougarae and Totiakton
were but cinder heaps. It had been demonstrated that
their country could be invaded and destroyed, and that
they who were masters of attack when in the enemy's
domain, scarcely knew how to defend their own homes
when foes in force equipped with firearms appeared.
It was then that they appealed to the English for protection. In November, 1687, the English King received
the Five Nations as "his subjects" and hostilities against
them were forbidden. It is greatly to be doubted that
any of the Iroquois knew what the term "subjects"
meant. They jealously held themselves independent,
but reserved the right to act as allies and be considered
as such. To have accepted the status of "subjects,"
even though pressed by great distress, was unthinkable
to them, and the English never sought to explain the
term employed in describing them.

Excavations in Seneca Village Sites. Years have
flown by and the stains of battle have been erased. The
waiting forest sprang up again and covered these ancient
town sites. The Yankee settler cleared the land and
laid out his farms and his villages. Then when the
twentieth century dawned, the archaeologist with
his spade and trowel came to uncover the buried
evidences of Seneca occupation and material culture.
All these old sites have been excavated and made to
reveal their secrets. Frederick Houghton, Edmund C.
Kelly, Alvin H. Dewey, Samuel P. Moulthrop, Walter
Cassebeer, Harrison C. Follett and other members of
the New York State Archeological Association have
sought for the buried history in these Seneca towns.

The writer, himself, has opened scores of ancient refuse pits and tombs in this Genesee country. In 1919-20, Gannagaro was explored and many beautiful specimens recovered, including three antler combs upon which were carved representations of the French and Dutch. The writer has spent many a week camping on these beautiful spots, and has dreamed the old scenes until it seemed as if he were living the old life again. Then, to bring a rude awakening a high-powered automobile would draw up at his tent and call attention to an aeroplane race passing by overhead. So has time wrought its changes. When the Seneca buried their slain, who could have predicted that men in the sky would look down into their re-opened graves!

But the Seneca had other reasons for seeking revenge. It will be remembered that Louis had requested that Iroquois captives be sent to France as galley slaves. Captives were sent as directed, and the French and their allies by many stern acts showed that they were determined to subdue the Iroquois. This brought about an equally determined resistance.

Iroquois Revenge. Moved by these insults, the Iroquois drew together for revenge, raising the cry that there should be no peace until their enslaved brothers should be freed. The bloody war of 1689 followed, when nine hundred Iroquois beseiged Fort Frontenac, though they did not take it. Then they invested Montreal, capturing three hundred to four hundred prisoners. In one battle lasting an hour they killed two hundred French soldiers and habitans. Later at Lachine one thousand five hundred Iroquois for two days ravished the country without opposition. During November that year one hundred and fifty warriors returned to Montreal where they killed all in their path and took a small fort. It was not until October that Frontenac returned with the galley slaves, at which the

Iroquois ceased their hostility for a few months. Winter and a scourge of smallpox were upon them with all their allied bitterness.

11.   The Dutch and English Establish Contact.

The years dragged on bringing misery to the French, and sapping the life blood of the Iroquois, who had no friends in all the world.   Yet, the Seneca and their allies stoutly maintained their independence and superiority as a race, fighting as "Men of Men" rather than submit to ignominious defeat.

English Penetration.   The English and their Dutch friends were now beginning to penetrate the Iroquois country and to spread their influence.   Before this the Indians had generally come to Albany for their councils. By 1698 the English began to awaken to what the French had long clearly seen,—the necessity of having forts and agents in every Iroquois canton.

On April 21, 1699, Captain John Schuyler, Captain John Bleeker, John Baptist VanEpps and Arnout Cornelisse Viele set out for Onondaga, as agents of the British interests, and reached the capital of the Iroquois League on April 28.   A council was held and the French wampum belts "kicked out"; the proposals of the English were accepted, the Iroquois agreeing to come to Albany to carry on further discussions.   They kept their word and at the Albany council of June 13, 1699, agreed that the English might build a fort in their midst and send a minister to them that they might learn the religion of England.   Thus ended the important events of the seventeenth century.   The Iroquois were revenged and the English were established among them as their allies and protectors.   What was now before them?   This another century was destined to reveal.

III. MATERIAL CULTURE AND SOCIAL ORGANIZATION OF THE SENECA.

Tribal Ideals. The Seneca, in common with their confederates, were a people of positive ideals and purposes. Their outlook was directed toward definite goals of accomplishment. Unlike the vegetating tribes about them, their belief was that a nation should function and attain certain desirable things. The very structure of the Iroquois Confederacy was built up on ideals, which, whether true or false, were nevertheless ideals, many of which were of amazing loftiness.

1. The Clan System.

We can scarcely understand Seneca history unless we know something about the ideals, beliefs, social customs and system of consanguinity, held by the group. Each tribe or nation was divided into clans, but the same clans, save three, were not found among all the nations. The Mohawk, for example, had only the Turtle, Bear and Wolf, while the Seneca had these three, and besides, the Beaver, Deer, Snipe, Heron and Hawk, and perhaps the Ball or Potato,—the latter being probably the clans of adopted captives. All the clans had certain heraldic devices by which they were distinguished.

The Clan Groups. The clan was a matrilinear family or group of families having a common symbol and meeting in a common council. The clan symbol is sometimes referred to as a *totem*, and it was probably believed in early times that the ancestress of the clan had this symbol as the object to which she and her descendants might make a fetichistic appeal. The clan was a political family, or a civil unit, and had the right, as such a unit, to own the personal property and the rights of its deceased members. It had the right to nominate civil chiefs and of deposing them; it had the right of revenging the injury of one of its number, of torturing captives or of adopting them; it had the right of burying its dead in a common ground, and of assembling the living in civil or religious councils.

Rights and Duties. The right of nomination was vested in a certain group of blood-related females, who when an office became vacant were convoked by the Name-holding matron to discuss a candidate. Often the men's council met for the same purpose, but the choice of the women usually prevailed. The national council then confirmed the nomination and when the new civil chief sat for the first time in the confederate council his name was confirmed by it.

The duty of the civil chief, as an officer of the clan and of the nation, was to concern himself with the welfare, internal peace of the clan and nation, to conserve the clan traditions, to maintain the dignity and rights of his clan and his office, and to represent his clan in national councils, and his nation in confederate councils. A clan chief, as a civil officer could not bear arms or go to war. To do this he had to vacate his office.

The whole structure of the League of the Iroquois was so devised that it made war officially a difficult thing to wage. There was, however, one exception to the rule of non-participation in war by a civil chief, in the person of Skunniwundi, who was a war and a civil chief. The Seneca had the right of supplying the two principal war captains in the persons of Ta-wan-ne-ahs and So-no-so-wa, respectively, and they had a seat and a voice in the national councils, but the two could only vote as one.

Iroquois Names. The right of bestowing names upon its members was distinctly a clan right, on the theory that a clan "owned" its constituents, and that the clan itself was the individual,—the member being only one of its composing units. Clans, therefore, had elaborate ceremonies for bestowing names, and might change them as the "name-holders" if the clan saw fit. There were lists of children's names, adult names, officers' names, civil names, etc., and a man's name might be taken from him at any time, for cause, and bestowed upon another. *Iroquois names were not descriptive of personal traits.* These names were not thought of as descriptions in any sense, and to translate an Iroquois name and then puzzle over its application or meaning is just as futile as to translate the name of Longfellow, Greenleaf, Hogson, Oyster, Axletree, Younghusband, Steinmetz, Taylor, Baker, Cook, Fuller, Smith, or Carpenter. We think of these appellations as names only, and thus it was with the Iroquois. Such names as Cornplanter, Red Jacket, etc., however, were bestowed by the white settlers, as descriptive of certain characteristics of these men.

Names of Civil Chiefs. Thus, in listing the names of the Seneca civil chiefs, no thought must be given to the meaning of the name, though for convenience we have added the English equivalent. Basing our nomenclature and spelling upon that of Lewis H. Morgan (which is not the modern scientific orthography), the list follows:

1. Ga-ne-o-di-yo (Handsome Lake), Wolf Clan, adopted by Turtles.
2. Sa-da-a-no-wus (Level Heavens), Snipe Clan.
3. Ga-no-gi-e (He Threatens), Turtle Clan.
4. Sa-geh-go-wa (Great Forehead), Hawk Clan.
5. Sa-de-a-no-wus (He-Helps-to-Hold), Bear Clan.
6. Nis-ha-ne-a-nent (Falling Day), Snipe Clan.
7. Ga-no-go-e-da-we (Hair Burned Off), Snipe Clan.
8. Do-ne-ho-ga-weh (Open Door), Wolf Clan.

In the consideration of this list, there are several points of considerable interest. It will be noted that

each clan was not entitled to a chief eligible to sit in the
national council. We note that the Snipe Clan had
three national chiefs, the Wolf had two, and the Turtle,
Bear and Hawk one each. The Beaver, the Heron and
the Deer are entirely left out. In this there is material
for certain considerations. It might be inquired whether
or not the Seneca tribe at the time of its formation did
not consist principally of a group of Snipe and Wolf
clansmen.

Names of the Clans. The Mohawk-Oneida group,
it will be found upon investigation, had only the Wolf,
Turtle and Bear, while the Onondaga group, which
came down from the north in advance of the Mohawk,
had these clans and also the Beaver, *Eel*, Snipe and *Ball*.
The Cayuga, who without much doubt grew out of the
Seneca group after its coming into Western New York,
had the same clans as the Seneca, except for the Heron,
but in the place of this clan it had the *Eel*.

Morgan lists the Wyandot clans as follows: Wolf,
Bear, Beaver, Turtle, Deer, *Snake*, *Porcupine* and Hawk.
Thus they, too, were similar to the Seneca, save for two
clans. Does it not seem to mean that the importance of
some clans, and the lack of others, that the absorption
of large bodies of captives led to the formation of new
clans, and also that certain clans divorced themselves
from the parent body and assisted in constituting new
groups? Does it not also seem that we must consider
the Iroquois in two groups,—the one having only the
three clans, and the other with the eight?

Seneca Names. In common with other nations of
the Huron-Iroquois family, the Seneca had complete
lists of clan names of several classes, and so familiar
were they with the type of name and its allusion that no
well informed Indian had difficulty in recognizing to
what clan a person belonged, once his name was heard.
Difficulty only occurred when a clan matron adopted a

Plate 10. Joseph Brant (Thayendanagea). War Captain of the
Mohawk Nation, a Mohawk of unalloyed lineage, British agent under
Sir William Johnson and uncompromising friend and supporter of the
Crown cause. Joseph Brant was born in 1742 and died in 1807.

child by clan rites. The name then temporarily went to the adopting clan, as it did in the case of Handsome Lake, the Seneca prophet, who, though born a Wolf, was adopted during his infancy by the Turtles and reared by them. The clan from which the person demitted, if it agreed, placed the wampum name-necklace in the hands of the adopting clan matron, trusting to her or her successor, to return it when the adopted person died. When Handsome Lake died his name-necklace, (ceremonially called "horns of office") was taken from his coffin, not by the Wolves who were entitled to it, but by the Turtles, who thus virtually confiscated it and re-employed it by "raising up" a successor to the name.

Laws of Custom. The clan no less than the nation compelled obedience to its customs and its edicts by social pressure, and woe to anyone who offended any of the laws of custom, or the mandates of council. There were no houses for punishment, no police. The standard of behaviour was enforced by means of ostracism and by social persecution. Anxious to fit into the scheme of things, to gain respect and to hold the regard of his fellows, the offender mended his manners before some irate warrior slew him as an enemy of the social body. Indeed, any person might kill or maim an offender of tribal customs who had been held up to public odium. Even a chief might be assassinated after the women had given him three warnings. Such executions were not revenged. In this manner the social integrity of the tribe was preserved; it was kept uniform by eliminating the anti-social. Such was the primitive jurisprudence of the Seneca dominion, and the doctrines of old have been preserved among the Seneca people to this day.

2. Seneca Cults and Societies.

Among the Seneca, as among their confederates, there were many ceremonial associations. Some of these were known to the people but others performed their rites apart from the non-initiate. Many of the societies and companies held public rites at the midwinter thanks-

Fig. 6. Interior of a Seneca bark lodge. Note how the sleeping compartments were curtained off. Note also the interesting framework of pole supports.

giving when they performed their dances and dramas for the benefit of the populace.

Seneca Cults. Each cult claimed to hold a supernatural formula by which certain spirits or forces of nature might be invoked and required to come to the assistance of the cult. These societies were reported to possess certain charms and fetiches which were propitiated at regular intervals. The rites of these organizations were in honor of the guardian spirits or heroes for which the society was named. No person was ever asked to become a member. All came of their own free will and accord, and were initiated when they had been found well qualified and worthy. Generally, a conjurer told the candidate which society he should join, or the novice would dream that he should become a member and then make application.

Among the well-known associations were the Company of Bears, the Otters' society, the Sisters of the Sustainers of Life, the Talkers with the Spirits, the False Face Company, the Society of the Great Sharp Point (Mystic Animals), and several others, fourteen in all, including the Ancient Guards of the Mystic Potence, sometimes called the Little Water Company or Grand Medicine Lodge of the Night Song (Ganoda).

This society has received a certain prominence due to its alleged similarity to the Masonic rites. Its ceremony has three sections, performed in total darkness, and the spirits of the animals who established it are supposed to return and make their presence known and felt in the gloom of the smoke-filled lodge. The hero of this society was slain by enemies who demanded the secret of his power. Then the creatures of the forest whom he befriended found him, and sacrificed their lives that the life-essence of their beings might enter the body of the hero and restore him to life. This done, those who remained behind to help composed their ritual and sang it until it entered the mind of the hero. Then the Bear which stood at his feet grasped his hand, raised him to life.*

In this ceremony the rushing sound of the cataract which the hero crossed is imitated by the shaking of gourd rattles, while the story of the society is chanted by the members. When morning comes, the members are given portions of the feast which had been cooked and depart with their pails of food. Usually this consists of boar's head and hulled corn hominy.

3. Games and Pastimes.

Fraternal societies and ceremonial associations did much to knit the clans, tribes and even the Confederacy itself into a cohesive whole, but an evaluation of the influence of sports and games must not be neglected. There were many popular games, and all who possessed physical ability entered into them with eagerness. The Seneca loved their pastimes and out-of-door sports, for they had been assured by their religious teachers that these games were pleasing to the Great Spirit. To play games and to enjoy athletic skill were, therefore, regarded as a part of religion.

Favorite Games. Among the favorite summer games of skill were Lacrosse, Crotch-and-Crook-stick, Hoop-and-Javelin, the Rolling-stone contest and archery; and during winter, snowshoe races, football, shinney, ice-ball, snow snake and whipping-top. Foot races were always popular. Gambling games, as platter-dice, and plumpits, were usually played in winter. The moccasin and jack-straw games were sometimes played for amusement. Besides these there were many minor children's games and pastimes. Education, indeed, was regarded as a game.

Games of skill and even gambling were often played

*A fuller account of these ceremonies is contained in the "Code of Handsome Lake, the Seneca Prophet," State Museum Bulletin, 163.

by one phratry, or one clan, against the other, while lacrosse, racing and archery were sometimes used as inter-tribal games. One of the most terrible games or tests of courage was the gauntlet which preceded an adoption, and we have the examples of Horatio Jones and VanCampen as gauntlet runners who won out. The gauntlet was a symbol of birth.

Dances. Besides games there were numerous dances which occurred upon the summons of the dance leaders. These were held in the long house or upon a suitable green. Morgan shows that there were fourteen dances in which men and women both participated, —seven for females alone and eleven for men. The "joined hands," in honor of the bean vines, was the only dance a person of one sex touched the other, but even this was discontinued by command of the religious leaders in recent times, who thought that it might lead strange men to tear the rings from the fingers of their dancing partners. Among the most popular of dances were the Pigeon dance, the Trotting dance, the Fish dance and the Joined Hands. Women were fond of the shuffle dances in which nimbleness of foot and grace of gesture gave play to skill and rhythm. The men for excitement liked the War dances, the Eagle dance, and the Stick Striking dance. After the dances favorite foods were doled out by the feast makers, and either eaten on the spot or carried home in suitable receptacles. Dances were regulated by Feastmakers (Ho-non-di-ont), or Officers of stated Ceremony. It was not for them to command or to exercise arbitrary authority, but to see that the requirements and taboos were not infringed. In this. as in all Iroquoian affairs, what a group of people wanted to do became the thing to do, always providing it was a legal desire, sanctioned by custom. It was a primitive *Vox populi, Vox Dei*, but the Vox Dei could not be perverted.

4. Temperamental Traits.

The Seneca were not a gloomy people but, to the contrary, a people who were fond of being excited. They enjoyed humor and jokes, and life in a Seneca town was lightened by the telling of humorous tales, and the playing of good natured jokes. When a stranger appeared, however, all was suppressed and the women moved with stately decorum; the children appeared shy, and the warriors posed in august dignity, not a smile appearing, though they might be bursting with internal laughter at the perplexity of the stranger. This is one of the principal reasons why most historians say that the Indians were taciturn, gloomy and given to austerity. They could not understand that even Indians had "company manners," nor did they know that the Seneca were commonly given to jesting and even punning. Many of their jokes were based upon manifestly absurd hyperboles, not dissimilar to those that even now cause us to smile. Satire and taunts were reserved for public speeches and for opponents in games. It was customary for friends to joke with one another, but no sane man might joke with his mother-in-law, or any elderly blood relative. There were even ceremonial dances where at each pause a man would step from the lines and tell a jovial story about a dancer on the other side of the line, at the same time presenting a gift of a trinket, a packet of tobacco or ball of maple sugar, to the common store, that no offense might arise.

The Seneca had all the fundamental desires of humanity. He loved his children, wanted a happy home, desired to exercise the powers within him to rank well among his fellows. To attain his hopes he knew the value of industry; life and safety he early discovered depended upon a settled life and upon an abundance of food. Hunting was a precarious business, and thus the Seneca learned to cultivate fields of food plants whereby his food supply might be near at hand. Above all traits the Seneca was patient, seeking revenge only when pressed beyond endurance.

5. Seneca Agriculture.

Garden Produce. With the Seneca the principal garden produce was corn, beans, squashes, melons, tobacco and sunflowers. These were grown in extensive communal fields, in which the clanswomen were required to work under the direction of a field matron. She regulated the work and supervised the singing and rest periods, when games were played or stories told. The men did the first rough work of clearing and burning, the women did the hoeing, and according to the times, it was a just division of labor. The products of the communal fields were stored in clan granaries and pits, but any individual might have his own garden and reserve its fruits for himself, always providing that a clansman might take what he needed for immediate purposes, if he announced the fact. Otherwise to take from a neighbor's private garden was regarded as thievery.

The Seneca had more than a dozen varieties of corn, and cultivated them with studious care, even understanding that species planted too closely together would "visit and establish colonies" on the cobs of their neighbors. They had several varieties of squashes and melons, and ten or more varieties of beans. They grew sunflowers for the oil which they expressed from the seeds. There were many wild foods which needed no cultivation, but which were gathered in great quantities. These included pond-lily roots, cattail roots, artichoke tubers, wild leek, mushrooms, lichens, and many varieties of nuts and berries.

The Seneca cook had many recipes for preparing her vegetable dishes, and corn was prepared in a score of palatable ways, among them corn soup, gruel, hominy, samp, hulled corn, corn bread, corn pudding and parched corn meal. These corn foods were mixed with beans and berries, nuts, and sunflower oil. Iroquois corn culture was a well developed thing, and it exercised a powerful influence upon their social and economic life. It compelled industry and thrift, and was largely responsible for a sedentary village existence. This was true of all the Huron-Iroquois.*

So vital were the fields to the Seneca people, and so largely did their whole life depend upon agriculture that when the French punitive expeditions desired to harass the Seneca they would swoop down upon them and destroy their corn-fields and burn their storehouses. This was killing by indirection, and it was seldom successful.

6. Seneca Village Life.

Seneca Houses. The villages of the Seneca clusters were of bark lodges, store houses, and other outer buildings. Houses were built on frameworks of poles and small tree trunks, covered with the bark of the elm, basswood or hemlock. The elm bark lodge was considered best. Great sheets of bark were removed from the trees during the late May and up to mid-July and preserved or used immediately for covering purposes. These were sewed to the frame of the lodge, not up and down, but horizontally. This insured a long enough stretch to permit the cribbing poles to hold the bark in place; besides, if the bark were hung up with the natural run of the grain, it had a tendency to curl up, but when hung sideways it straightened out flat. Bark lodges were from twelve to eighteen feet high and from about eighteen to two hundred in length, depending upon the character of the structure. On either side of

*For a general treatise on Iroquois agriculture and foods, see Iroquois Uses of Maize and Other Food Plants, by A. C. Parker, Bulletin 144, New York State Museum.

Plate 11. (Upper) Seneca masks used in the False Face Ceremony. (Lower) Masks used by the Ha-dih-dos company.

Fig. 7. Exterior of Seneca bark lodge. The Seneca communal long lodge was frequently more than 150 feet in length and held several families.

the interior were long bunks, one above the other like the upper and lower beds in a sleeping car. The lower bunks were used as lounging places during the day and the upper platforms as storage shelves for dishes, dried food, pelts and other portable property. The lower platforms could be curtained off so as to give privacy to the sleepers at night. Through the center of the lodge ran a long hallway in the middle of which were the fires, so arranged at intervals that one fire served a set of four compartments. The smoke escaped through a hole in the roof, the draft being regulated by opening or closing one of the doors at the extremities of the lodge. On the supporting timbers rested long poles that hung just over the line of the upper platforms. Upon these were suspended numerous braids of trussed corn, hanks of herbs, dried pumpkins and squashes, and occasionally hanks of dried tobacco. Each compartment was a sacred place and not to be violated by another. The space beneath the lower beds was sometimes boxed in, making a storage vault below. In this were kept personal treasures and stores. For anyone but the owner to pry into these was a grave offence. Thus, while the Seneca lived in a communal way they still had private ownership and the right of personal privacy. There were rights that were sacredly individual.

Children. Children were greatly loved and they swarmed the Seneca towns. The coming of a child was an occasion of rejoicing, and girls were even more welcome than boys, since the female occupied an honored place. Nevertheless, each family had only as many children as it could properly care for, which was seldom more than three, even birth control being a right of mothers. If there were too many or they became orphaned, children were placed in the care of those who had few children or none. It was the rule that the control of life should be in the hands of the women and they deemed it best to bear children only when the last child was able to walk and in a measure care for himself, which was at about the age of four or five. By this method every baby had its mother's undivided attention, a most necessary thing under the conditions of life in which they lived. Too many babies meant danger when raids occurred.

Children were schooled by their elders in such a way that they learned by experience rather than by admonition. They would be told that to play in the fire would cause the fire demons to "bite" them. The child might test this statement and find it true, but he did not do so because someone had said, "Don't do it". When children reached the age of twelve they were placed under the leadership of certain elderly "guides" for instruction. It was a primitive Boy Scout system of development. Girls clung more closely to their mothers, but even they had their associations.

7. Rights of Seneca Women.

Women's Rights. Houses and land belonged to the women, for the right of ownership descended in the mother line. This gave Iroquois women* advantage over the men in many ways. So important was an Iroquois woman that, when captured by the enemy, it required twice the ransom to redeem her that it did a man. Domestic life was entirely controlled by the

---

*The Seneca do not use the term "squaw". With them it is a term of disrepute and is regarded as an obscene appellation. A Mohawk woman some years ago explained to the British agent who addressed the women as "squaws," that this term with them meant "mons veneris". This is due to the similarity of the Iroquoian term to the Algonkian squaw, meaning a married woman. A Seneca once stated that as he would not call an European woman a wench or huzzy (though this was good English in Shakespeare's time), so he did not wish his women called squaws. The term is in disrepute among all Indians today and they generally regard it as insulting.

women, and they were regarded as the heads of the household; the men were only the meat providers, the defenders and law makers.

Men's Duties. Women were also the mistresses of the vegetable supplies, and they gathered the harvest, but to the men fell the heavier task of bringing in the flesh of the forest. This was no light task, for it entailed carrying heavy burdens for long distances. Explorers and missionaries have left us the record that the hunters often became injured and worn out with their heavy tasks, and that they frequently succumbed to exhaustion on the trails. Hunting and fishing in those days were not a sport or a pastime, but a serious business fraught with danger and uncertainty. Enemies prowled the forests seeking to trap unwary hunting parties. It was thus necessary for men to rest upon their arms continually in order to preserve their villages from sudden attack.

8. Religion of the Seneca.

Religion. Religion played a vital part in the life of the Seneca people. It might be concluded that religion pervaded everything and regulated all the habits of the people, for most of their customs and their daily behavior were controlled by religious beliefs. There were numerous observances and ceremonies, all of which were deemed essential, but even so, religious freedom was basic. So long as one did not violate the fundamental taboos,—things forbidden by long standing customs,—he might worship as he wished and call upon his own particular totems in his own way. The Iroquois never waged war over matters of religion, or to compel people to believe as they did, neither did they ever torture their captives in order to force them to acknowledge the gods of their pantheon. Their war upon missionaries was not because of religion.

Like the Greeks, the Iroquois had many gods, but these were regarded more as unseen beings belonging to the primal order. It has been said that the Iroquois did not have a principal god until after the coming of the Jesuits who gave them the idea, and this may be true, but it is also true that their gods ranked in importance, some being under the direction of others in the capacity of agents or subordinates, as with the Greeks.

Cosmology. The chief of the god-beings was Earth Holder (Tehaohwenjaiwahkonh) who ruled the sky-world and lived in a great white lodge beneath the spreading branches of the celestial tree in the middle of the heavens. His consort was the Great Mother, called Yagentji, whom the Jesuits said the Hurons called Ataentsic. Through her curiosity to see what was beneath the celestial tree, she caused it to be uprooted, to the amazement and wrath of her husband, who thrust her into the hole through the sky made by the root cavity of the tree. Down she fell to be received upon the wings of the water birds. The under-sea turtle rose from the waters beneath, and a muskrat diving to the bottom of the ocean brought up a bit of earth which he deposited on the turtle's shell, causing it to grow large enough to receive the woman. The turtle waxed large and the earth increased until a large growing island was formed. The sky-woman brought life with her and shortly gave birth to a daughter who immediately grew to maturity and began to help her mother. The daughter circumambulated the island each day, and upon a certain occasion while swinging upon a vine she was united to an unseen lover. In due season she gave birth to two boys, one of whom caused her death. The sky-woman directed the elder boy to bury his mother and watch over her grave. Indeed, she required him to do much work, and petted the younger boy as a favorite. The elder boy was known as the Light One or Good Mind and the younger as the Dark One or Evil Mind.   Good Mind watched over his mother's grave and watered it as directed.   From the soil over her breasts sprang the maize plant, giving sweet milk from its kernels for the nourishment of her children.   From her body sprang the squash, from her fingers the bean plant, from her forehead the tobacco plant and from her toes the artichokes and other edible tubers.

It was not long before Good Mind sought his father, and after a long perilous journey over the eastern sea found him on a mountain top.   He was put to tests by which he was compelled to overcome whirlwinds, flames, great falling rock-masses and the current of the cataract. The great shining being at the mountain top then acknowledged him as his son and announced, "I am your father".   The being was the Sun.

Here is a beautiful allegory in which the Seneca was taught that life came to earth from celestial realms, that to be good-minded one must labor, that as the seed dies in giving life to the living plant so through trials and victory over obstacles and temptation man finds his supreme father.

When Good Mind returned, he brought with him pouches filled with all manner of birds, fish, mammals and plants.   These escaped at the proper time and became the progenitors of the living things of earth. The myth goes on to relate that Good Mind and Evil Mind had a contest, in which, by betrayal of confidence, Evil Mind sought to slay Good Mind with deer antlers. Evil Mind was then banished to the under-earth world and took with him his evil creatures, there to dwell forever.

Good Mind in due season created human beings out of the reflection of himself which he saw in a pool of water, molding this reflection into the clay in human form.   He then became invisible and returned to the heaven-world over a celestial path formed by a ray of light,—his grandmother, the sky-woman, departing with him. This beneficent earth-god was called by the Seneca, Thahonhiawahkon, but he is mentioned in the literature of the Jesuit fathers, who wrote on the mythology of the Hurons, as Iousheha. He is also called Hahnigoio, and his evil brother Hahnegoetga.

Belief in Spirits. The Whirlwind and the Thunderer were also gods and there were gods of dreams, of death, and of other natural forces. These were conceived rather as spirits who might be propitiated and honored, but who had no creative power other than certain magical ability to transform things. The Sun was chief among the spirits of nature, ruling the day, the Moon governed the night, the Morning Star heralded the dawn, the Zephyr brought health, and the Spirits of Sustenance made the food plants grow.

Mysterious beings lived in the air and in the forest's depths, but, likewise, there were also evil monsters with frightful powers. In the sky dwelt the good Ohshadahgea, the Cloud Land Eagle, always ready to rescue the perishing. A dew-pool rested between his shoulders, and when the rain did not fall he gave drink to the thirsty plants. Under the waters dwelt the Horned Snake, who, while a magical creature, committed no evil other than to appear in human form to woo and lure away unsuspecting maidens to his underwater caverns. The Horned Snakes loved human wives, but the Thunderer hated the whole tribe and fought them whenever they appeared above the waves.

Fairies. The Seneca believed in fairies and pygmies, and many are the tales of these tiny people who were friendly to man. Some of the pygmies lived in rocky glens as at the upper falls of the Genesee,* and

---

*The Senecas believed that a tribe of fairies lived beneath each fall at Letchworth Park.

others under the water. Another tribe lived in the
woods and had as its task the turning of the face of
fruit so that it would ripen in the sun. These "little
folk" were unable to do many things for themselves and
gave favor in exchange for services rendered them by
their human friends. They asked that small bags of
tobacco be thrown over the cliffs for them and that boys
and girls often trim their finger nails, so that they could
use the parings to frighten away bad animals, for the
nails smelled like human beings and thus the animals
became afraid. Often when they needed human help,
they would be heard drumming in the glens, and this
was always a signal that mankind should hold a dance
for them and sing pygmy songs.

Giants. Giants were believed to dwell in the
mountains among the rock cliffs. These giants were
called Stone Coats because they could not be killed by
spear thrusts or arrows, for their skins were as hard as
stone. They sought to hunt down men and women and
eat them raw. At last all the giants were chased into a
cave near Onondaga and the Thunderers shook down
the rocks upon them. Some say that one lone survivor
imparted his wisdom to a frightened boy, who had
sought refuge in his cave, and so transmitted his wisdom
through the False Face Company, which he commanded
the boy to organize. The company has in one of its
secret ceremonies a great mask covered with pebbles
and having a flint arrow point imbedded in its forehead.
The hair is shredded bark, for it was not human and
therefore could have no real hair. The present writer
once collected such a mask and placed it in the State
Museum.*

---

*For a full description of the myths and folklore of the Seneca see
"Seneca Myths and Folklore," by Parker, published by the Buffalo
Historical Society, 1924.

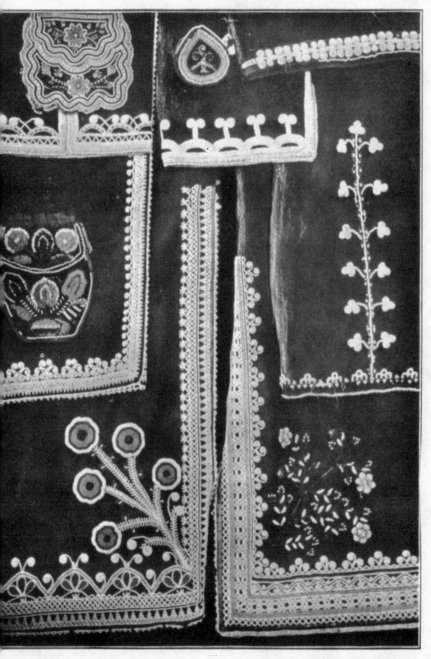

Plate 12. Decorations and ornamentation on Seneca garments
(Period 1750-1850).

9. Basic Beliefs of the Seneca.

The fundamental belief of the Seneca was in the existence of a Great Power that pervaded all nature. This concept does not seem at first to have been well defined, but it is the root of the belief in folk-spirits. Later it matured into a belief in Haweniu as the supreme God. This name means "The Great Good Voice" and is a deification of all power and the creative good in nature.

The Unseen World. In common with the other Iroquois the Seneca conceived of numerous unseen spirits that lived in everything and were capable of manifesting themselves to man. It was believed that every atom in nature was intelligent. For this reason it was deemed proper for men to talk to the rocks, the winds, the trees and the waters. Even a clod of soil had life and consciousness, for the Creator had thought it into being. It was therefore believed that all things had souls of greater or lesser intensity, and that there was an unspoken language, emanating from the heart, that all understood. Cases were cited to show that far-away friends could transmit their thoughts, and that men by thinking could cause other men as well as animals to obey them. It was deduced that there was an unseen and all-powerful Master of Souls into whose keeping all departed souls went for refuge, and who assisted the living to find mystical power.

The Seneca believed that Good and Evil were in a condition of constant warfare, but that Good should triumph, and Evil perish no matter how much power it had acquired. It was believed that men and women could acquire magical power from the spirits of good or evil, and so become magically powerful for good, or become Wizards for evil. Good magic was called "orenda," and evil, "otgont".

It was their belief that it was possible for one creature to transform itself into other beings. As all living things are only the reflections of the Creator, reflection is the real substance of things, but, as a reflection is not material substance, it might easily be transmuted or transplanted into other forms. Thus a man who had acquired orenda might transform himself into a deer, or any other animal. Evil beings sought the reflection of evil and had the same power, but it was not believed to be enduring, for "otgont" power diminishes as it is used, but "orenda" grows stronger.

Ghosts were thought to be unhappy earth-bound spirits, who either wanted to settle some earthly affair, or who wandered over the earth because they were malicious and desired to do harm. Good spirits were thought to be able to conclude their earthly affairs in ten days, and then depart. As names were "cords or strings of attachment," it was not right to speak the real names of the dead, for fear of calling the souls back from pleasant abodes to the scenes of earthly conflict. Thus when a departed soul was mentioned, an implied name was mentioned, as "He-who-dwelt-by-the-cliff-and-made-good-bowls" or "She-who-had-a-bone-necklace-as-a-neck-ornament". Every man sought to have some personal trait or to do certain things, in order to have an implied name. Names were not revealed to strangers for fear that the stranger might conjure the name and perhaps work injury to the person.

Heaven. That there was a heaven was never doubted, for what could be more logical than to believe that the good should find immortality? Here the good went for regeneration, here the Creator shut the eyes of pilgrims and took their soul-bodies to pieces, putting them back joint by joint and sinew by sinew, until all evil and disease had been found and eliminated, leaving the soul-being regenerated and completely good. This remaking of souls was necessary since sin was believed to be a thing that could not be forgiven, but which polluted the soul. Upon concepts such as these the Seneca built his faith in the essential brotherhood of all life, his hope of immortality and his eternal salvation. If some of his practices were cruel and inhuman, it was because the Seneca, like his white brother, belonged to the "inhuman human race"; it was because his beliefs required him to satisfy the demons of war who craved suffering and blood. If this agony did not come from the enemy, it would be exacted from the friend. He was no more cruel than his European brother of the same period, who burned heretics alive, boiled them or flayed them or impressed them in "iron maidens". There is but one difference,—we remember the Indian's savagery, but we have forgotten our own.

Thanksgivings. The religion of the Seneca was one of thanksgiving. Each season had its thanksgiving ceremony in which the Creator and his subordinate spirits were thanked for their gifts. The Mid-winter ceremony, lasted nine days, during which the High Priest offered thanks for every object in nature, from the sands beneath the waters beneath the earth, to the celestial tree itself. At this ceremony the dancing associations, the fraternities and cults were called upon to give public exhibitions. All who had perplexing dreams were asked to tell them, that someone might give the right interpretation, and those who greatly desired some boon were given an opportunity to tell the "dream guessers". Then, all those who had sinned were asked to confess before all men and to promise to make restitution. They were then called upon to walk over a straight road in the snow, as a symbol of their repentance.

Springtime began with the maple festival and a thank offering to the sap and sugar that the tree afforded. Later came the Planting festival, followed in June by the Strawberry feast. In early autumn came the Corn Thanksgiving, and later the Festival of the Harvest. These celebrations were religious thanksgivings, but there was great merriment during the afternoon and evening dances, for to enjoy life was supposed to be an evidence that life was desired and that mankind was thankful for it. To live as if one were in perpetual fear of the Creator's wrath and to act as if life were a fearful burden, was thought an affront to the giver of life. The Seneca believed in making "a joyful noise unto the Lord," and in dancing before Him.

10. Material Culture.

Industry. The vigorous conditions of forest life called for constant industry. An indolent people could not exist and meet the requirements of nature and society. The Seneca were a busy and industrious people, and their houses and hamlets were filled with evidences of their industrial activity. They were not such simple folk who could live like the birds without tools, but on the other hand were fond of having implements and utensils for their housekeeping and their forest activities. As house-builders they hewed down trees with their stone axes, supplemented by fire; they cut logs for their stockades and hollowed out tree trunks for their dugouts. Their canoes, however, were generally of elm bark stretched and fastened over ash frames. They were good canoe makers, but were not essentially a water people, often suffering defeat from the Algonkian people when they fought water battles. Canoe-making required much industry, for there were the ribs, gunwales and paddles to make with stone and bone tools, for the Iroquois had no metal until the European period. They knew of native copper but would not use this emblem of their enemies. It was one of their taboos, and a strange one, for when the European came they eagerly adopted it, finding that the all-powerful invader was made prosperous by it.

Men's Work. Men manufactured snowshoes, lacrosse sticks, stone and pottery pipes and also various knives and points of chert. They manufactured implements from antler, bone and shell,—as awls, combs, beads and pendants. They were workers in wood, and

Fig. 8. Man's ear with silver wound rim.

carved out bowls and spoons, baby-carrying cases and other household utensils. They gathered elm and basswood bark for ropes and cords, but the women took the raw material and manufactured it. Men hunted the pelts and shared with the women in tanning them for clothing and moccasins. Women did most of the sewing and manufactured the hunting shirts and leggins, even to embroidering them with moosehair and porcupine quills, sometimes in color. Naturally, the men caught the porcupines and pulled out the quills, but the women sorted the quills and dyed them. The Seneca tailoress cut the deer skins evenly, trimming off the neck and leg projections, and fringing the edges by incising them with a sharp flint chip. The men preferred to make their own hats. The Iroquois hat was a tightly fitting cap from the top of which a flurry of feathers floated, one splendid plume whirling from a spindle at the top. The Iroquois did not wear a bonnet of erect feathers like the Sioux of the open plains. Such was out of place in the forest; erect feathers would catch in the trees and shrubs through which they passed. Artists of a modern date often forget this.

The men made the corn mortars by cutting off logs and then making a hollow of sufficient depth by means of fire. Men also made the pestles, and each mortar was supposed to have two. Other wooden articles that men produced were bows, arrows, warclubs, ladders and troughs. Barrels and large bowls were made from elm bark by the men, but the women made the fabrics and baskets.

Loss and Waste. The house-life to the Seneca was one of constant activity, for utensils, tools and weapons were constantly wearing out and had to be replaced. A great source of attrition was the sacrifice of weapons, arrows, dishes and ornaments to the spirits of the animals whom they had killed for food. When these articles were of stone, clay, antler, bone or other enduring substance, they were preserved in the refuse heaps, and today the archeologist finds them as mute evidence of the industry of the ancient. It is only because the Seneca of the historic period clung to their ancient material culture, that we are able to explain so much of their ancient civilization. Because of greater convenience they abandoned their clay kettles and pipes, and their bone, stone and shell ornaments for the brass trade-kettle, the kaolin pipe, the steel and iron knives and glass trade beads, but they did retain many of their ceremonial paraphernalia and games, and kept other implements as heirlooms.

Cultural Survivals. At the beginning of the twentieth century many of the Seneca and Onondaga know how to make cords of bark, ceremonial baskets, moccasins and masks of corn husks, to carve their ritualistic wooden masks, to make their ceremonial

Fig. 9. Seneca spoon of wood (½ size).

rattles, drums and whistles, and in the economic life some of the implements and utensils used in the preparation of their native corn for food; they still make and use, washing and sifting baskets, mortars, pestles, paddles, wooden spoons, bark trays and bowls and even burden straps woven from elm and basswood cords. Herein is evidence of the innate conservatism of the Seneca, who clings to that which he himself can make and understand. Cultural decay can only set in when he becomes an absolute dependent upon things which he cannot make. The material culture of the Iroquois had much to do with his preservation, for it was connected with his ceremonial and ritualistic life; it was a part of the folk-ways of the group which insisted, "This shalt thou do and not do otherwise".

An industry contributes to regularity, mutual consideration and thrift, an industrious people is an evidence of moral energy and mental acumen. The Seneca, however they may have differed from the Europeans in religious and moral beliefs, were not essentially immoral or irreligious. There were few precepts of an ethical nature that the missionaries could teach them, and they frequently resented the missionary attitude that they did not know what was essentially right and wrong.

Sophiology. While it is true that many of their beliefs and practices may appear as folly and superstition, once analyzed these same things may be found to contain beautiful and even lofty ideas. Ignorance of true causes often led to a perversion of what was otherwise good, and the symbol of good to be worshipped rather than the reality itself. This has happened in all religions, and Christianity, as we have modified it for our use, has retained many of the pagan ideas through which it has filtered, as any professor of theology will admit. It is but natural that the Iroquois should have gone afield in some things, but, after all, there is in their religion a certain stately beauty and sublimity that is inspiring. If these people have transgressed against our code, they were but following the teachings and

Plate 13. Red Jacket. Red Jacket was the famous Seneca orator and councilor. He was not a civil chief, though as a war chief he led a company of warriors in the War of 1812, and had the rank of Captain.

example of nature itself, and were therefore unmoral in such matters rather than immoral, but how shall we pass judgment or cast "the first stone"?

Let us consider that the Seneca (uncontaminated by unwholesome European influence, and unspoiled by the lust which love of gain awakened within their souls) were a people who believed in an all powerful Great Spirit, in the immortality of the soul, in a life-everlasting, and in the fraternity of all life. They believed that it was natural to be honorable and truthful, and cowardly to lie. With them a thankful heart was prayer; they did not seek to instruct The Great Spirit what to do on earth or in the celestial world, for they had faith that in his wisdom he knew what was right and best. "Such was the faith of the Seneca who would not insult his God by commanding him, or by fearing that he would not care for his people."

IV. A CENTURY OF DECULTURATION.

1700-1800.

1. The Choice of Allies.

A Complex Situation. The dawn of the eighteenth century found the Seneca disrupted by conflicting emotions and perplexed by the interplay of events over which they had no control. Jealous of their own sovereignty and domain, they saw both threatened by two powerful white rivals. With which should they cast their lot was a vital question. To ally themselves with France meant that they must forget many bitter grievances, and yet the French people pleased them more than all other Europeans. Frenchmen would live with them on terms of equality, adopt their manners, venture on war parties with them, and willingly marry their daughters. The individual Frenchman was a congenial companion. His colony asked only for the right to trade and, indeed, demanded that friendly Indians should trade only with Frenchmen. French missionaries were faithful and kind, but these same missionaries seemed to be the tools of political interests, and frequently carried away hosts of Christian converts to Canada, where they took up arms against their kinsfolk. Yet, after all, the Frenchman as an individual was a likable fellow, though his colonial policy was a menace.

The English. With their Dutch friends at Albany were the English. They seldom came among the Iroquois, asking rather that the Iroquois come to them. Englishmen assumed a haughty attitude and treated the Indians with an air of contempt. Besides this, the English were interested in acquiring great tracts of land, as was proven by their penetration of the Hudson and Mohawk valleys, and their control of New England, eastern Pennsylvania, New Jersey, Maryland, Virginia and Carolina. One point was in favor of the British; it was the fact that they did not want the French to lay hold of Iroquois lands, and were willing to assist by military force to prevent French incursions, but this was not enough to force a choice of masters. One factor alone should decide this: It was, *which nation could be depended upon to be most just in its dealing with the Iroquois?*

Upon the answer to this question depended not only the fate of the Iroquois, but the future control of North America. During the opening years of the eighteenth century the course of events was to answer the question and determine which nation should receive the support of the Iroquois people. Logically, it could not be the nation who had allied itself with the Huron.

2. The Influence of the Joncaires.

Joncaire. The Niagara region was a pivotal point, where was destined to be settled one of the decisive arguments affecting the future control of the Atlantic seaboard. Here, at the beginning of the century, is a remarkable Frenchman whose career commands our earnest attention. Upon him depended much of the hold which France was to have upon the region. He was Louis Thomas de Joncaire, the Sieur de Chabert, son of Antoine Marie and Gabriel Hardi,—born about 1670 (1668?), in the town of St. Remi in Arles, Provence. We do not know exactly when he came to America, but it is thought that he shipped with the Chevalier de Vaudreuil in 1687, for Vaudreuil afterwards appeared as his friend and defender. Joncaire's military attainments were not high, but he showed a singular business ability and an unusual capacity for making friends. Soon after he reached America he was a member of a small expedition of twelve men which was captured by a party of Seneca who planned to test the Frenchmen by torture. Some accounts say that all of his companions were tortured to death, and that Joncaire himself was made ready for the stake, but subsequent happenings seem to indicate that the French captives were only tested for their courage. Joncaire, so the story goes, was seized by his captor, who was about to tie his hands in preparation to scorch his fingers, when Joncaire set upon the Indian and gave him such a terrible beating that his nose was smashed and his face streamed with blood. The assembled Seneca whooped in approval at this display of courage and drew Joncaire to their bosoms as a companion and brother worthy of their protection.

It was five years before Joncaire and his companions were released, and Joncaire had improved every moment of his captivity to cement the Seneca as his friends. He learned the language, took part in their ceremonies and studied their oratory and council methods. He so proved his loyalty that the Seneca by all their ancient rites adopted him as a son, and raised him from the status of captive to that of recognized warrior, and then to rank of Sachem. When he was released in the autumn of 1694, he was thoroughly imbued with the philosophy of his Indian friends and with a sympathy for them that endured throughout his long life, and yet he never forgot that he was an emissary of France.

Though freed from captivity, Joncaire kept in touch with his red friends, and his peculiar capacity to deal with them led the King of France to order him to live with them again during the year 1705. This official return was the occasion of great rejoicing with the Seneca, who hailed him as a brother indeed. His presumably voluntary return was a coup for the French. For Joncaire they would do anything, even to sparing the lives of French captives.

3. The Contest for Niagara.

Claims on Niagara. At this time the French were
concerned with the fact that the Iroquois had deeded to
the English their beaver land north of the Great Lakes,
entering into a compact at the Albany Council of July
10, 1701. This was a gesture against Canada and
French control. It was also a threat at Niagara, the key
of the lower lakes. If the French could assemble the
power they were determined to possess themselves of
this key and to shut the door to rivals. Joncaire alone
could win the help of the Seneca, who held the key.
By every tradition Niagara belonged to New France,
for it was here in 1669 that LaSalle had built the ill-fated
Griffon, and here Denonville had constructed his fort
of 1687. Where the hand of France had been, there its
grip should stay, was the resolve.

For a number of years, the English had been
actively concerned in cementing the allegiance of the
Five Nations, and had been successful with all except
the Seneca. The Iroquois were a necessary barrier
between them and the French Canadians. As a further
protection, a fort and post were needed at Niagara. The
French anticipated this. In the hands of the British
this meant loss of trade and power to New France.
Thus, though the French had built no fort there, since
that of Denonville (which was abandoned the next
year), every year witnessed the attempts of French
traders to deal with the Indians at the mouth of the
Niagara. Joncaire appeared there in 1705, no doubt
hoping to open a post on his own account. The English
complained about this, having an eye upon Niagara
themselves. A confidential report to Louis XIV, sent
by his agent, who had been charged with the task of
inspecting all the French forts and posts on the Great
Lakes, read in part:

"His Majesty is informed that the English are endeavoring to seize the post at Niagara, and that it is of very great importance for the preservation of Canada to prevent them from so doing, because were they masters of it, they would bar the passage and obstruct the communication with the Indian allies of the French, whom as well as the Iroquois they would attract to them by their trade, and dispose, whenever they please, to wage war on the French. This would desolate Canada and oblige us to abandon it."

The Niagara Controversy. The advantages of controlling the Niagara frontier were apparent. With Niagara in their grip, the French had an all-water route to lower Canada, while the English were compelled to carry their pelts for the most part through the lands of the Seneca and their allies. Though LaSalle's "Griffon," launched in 1669, was the first deep bottomed boat built by the French for traffic, via Niagara and Ontario, it was also the last. French fur trade was borne by canoes. The English had other dreams,—dreams of commanding the routes, the lands and the people whence trade flowed.

The New York colony remonstrated again and again against the stultifying French occupation of Niagara, but received scant satisfaction, for the Iroquois answered that it was without their permission. Beyond this the Seneca adroitly stated that they could not *give* Niagara land to the English as requested since it was conquested territory and belonged to all the Iroquois nations. When it was remonstrated that Joncaire was there with a land grant, they asserted their right to allow one of their own sons and sachems to build a house where it pleased him. And it so happened that Joncaire, the elder (after a winter's sojourn among the eastern Seneca, who were most friendly to the English), hurried on to Niagara and, with his Indian colleagues, he took up an abode. During the next fifteen years, he was busy in the interests of Canada and, indeed, in building for himself a reputation as a trader.

Seneca Locations. The opening years of the eighteenth century found the Seneca again in a condition of readjustment. The blow of Denonville had forced them to abandon their old seats and take up new abodes. The eastern Seneca settled near Seneca lake in a large town south-west of the present site of Geneva, calling it Ganechstage, and in a smaller village at Onagee, just west of Canandaigua. As the country was now free from attack by hostile Indians, and as they now were becoming pelt hunters, they began to wander off in small bands to the south, and there were numerous small hamlets and camps in many out of the way places.

The Seneca of the western branch from Totiakton and Gannounonta, after taking refuge where they might in the forests to the south, began to settle along the Genesee or near it, particularly at Geneseo, though they built towns still further up the river. These Seneca, also, began to scatter, many of them wandering off into Pennsylvania and Ohio. Their normal life was altered and they, likewise, were giving up their fields and villages for a roaming hunter life. Civilization pressing upon them forced them backward in the scale of culture.

4. Political Problems of the Seneca.

Divisions of the Seneca. In the events that follow it will be noted that the western division of the Seneca were friendly to the French Canadians. It will appear that the Seneca nation was split by conflicting interests. History has not explained just why this was the case, but we may consider a possible explanation to be that the west-most villages of the Seneca were filled with adopted Huron and Neutral together with their children, now grown to maturity, and that these had natural reasons for being sympathetic toward the French,—the

allies of their ancestors.   We may thus understand that
while the eastern Seneca villages were friendly to the
English, those along the Genesee were wont to listen
to the voices of the French priests, traders and officials
from Montreal and Quebec.   It was a case where traditions and blood bore fruit, and it was a fruit that nearly
caused the "fall" of a nation.

Nevertheless, when the young warriors of the
Seneca were on hunting expeditions, enemies did not
discriminate; a Seneca was a Seneca.   Thus, the hostile
Ottawa in 1704 treacherously attacked a Seneca party
near Fort Frontenac (near the foot of Lake Ontario at
the beginning of the river St. Lawrence) and carried
away thirty prisoners in triumph to Detroit, where the
French commandant, seeing what had been done, demanded liberation instantly.   French allies might not
war upon each other.   The Iroquois were inflamed, and
in 1706 Joncaire was sent by Vaudreuil to Michilimack-
inack, to establish peace between these two hostile
forces, for French trade depended upon peace between
the fur producers.   It was during this year that the
Nanticoke brought tribute to Onondaga.   They were a
lower Susquehanna-Delaware tribe which had been
subjugated.

The Iroquois Lean toward England.   Though the
French did much to win the Iroquois, the English were
not asleep and the tribes east of the Seneca were
gradually taking advantage of opportunities to sell to
them, though the overland route for heavy packs of
peltries was not attractive.   By 1709, through the overtures of Peter Schuyler, patroon of Albany, all the
Iroquois save the Seneca were drawn to the side of the
English as allies and supporters, but the Mohawk and
Onondaga, fearing that the French might construe this
as a hostile act, sent word to Canada that they did not
move for war.   This year the captive tribes in Pennsyl-

Plate 14. Tee-yee-neen-ho-ga-row. This chief, whose Seneca name would be Do-ne-ho-ga-weh, was one of the Mohawk sachems of the Wolf clan who visited England in 1710. It is possible that he may have been a Seneca.

vania planned to go to Onondaga with their tribute, but the Governor objected that it was not a proper time. Later a council was held at Conastoga, attended by many Seneca. The Tuscarora appeared with belts of wampum, as an assurance of their desire for peace in their southern homeland in the Carolinas, for they had been in conflict with the colonists.

The Chiefs Visit England. In furtherance of the English designs, Colonel Schuyler had taken a number of Iroquois and Mohikan chiefs to England, that they might catch a glimpse of England's glory and power. The chiefs returned in 1710, having been graciously received by Queen Anne. Three years later the Treaty of Utrecht was signed between France and England, and it was agreed that England should have all authority over the Five Nations of the Iroquois, but that there should be no restraint of trade by either nation. This year, 1713, the English were asked to mediate between the warring Carolina Indians and the Tuscarora, the latter having been badly defeated in their stronghold and eight hundred of them taken prisoners were sold as slaves. The Tuscarora now began to come into Pennsylvania and creep into New York where they sought the shelter of their northern kindred.

The Catawba. The Iroquois began to experience considerable trouble with their vassals, and found it difficult to settle them in places where they would not make a disturbance. Groups of the western Seneca (who were undoubtedly Andaste and Erie united with the Shawnee and Delaware) caused serious apprehension. Enemy tribes in the south were causing commotion, the Catawba having murdered some wandering Iroquois. The Seneca went down the Susquehanna to punish the offenders and after being turned aside by the Pennsylvania authorities, proceeded and, after a battle, brought back a host of captives and the promise that the trouble would not be repeated. It was thus that Catawba-Sioux blood seeped into the Iroquois cantons.

5. French Maneuvers to Secure Niagara.

The Contest for Niagara. The year, 1720, came and with it a renewed attempt of the French to settle a post at Niagara. The Seneca now had a small village at Lewiston, where many earned wages as carriers on the portage around the river above the falls. Joncaire had wintered once more among the eastern Seneca near Seneca lake and at Onagee. He took back to Canada a great store of peltries, and now prepared to return with another supply of brandy, cloth and other staple articles. With young LaCorne, son of the Mayor of Montreal, he reached Niagara and built a large cabin of bark, setting up the armorial standard of France, and calling his building, "Magazin Royal". Leaving the place in the hands of LaCorne, he returned to Canada for new supplies. In the meantime an English emissary, Lawrence Classen, of Albany, went to Niagara and protested against the French domination of the Niagara portage, but was told that it was by command of the Governor of Canada. Later Classen went to Seneca Castle to protest, but the Seneca were induced by Joncaire, who appeared on the scene, to dispute with the English agent, affording a non-committal reply, though Classen made good his point that the French were charging them double for the goods they gave in exchange. Joncaire, with rare eloquence, smoothed out the trouble, promising that a French fort at Niagara meant much to the Seneca, and giving them presents in testimony of his friendship. Personality and an appeal to emotions had triumphed over reason; the Gaul was the victor over the Teuton, but the red American paid the bill.

Joncaire's victory was received with acclaim in

Canada and he was pronounced to be "the best man for Niagara," and his orders were to "pillage the English" if they appeared for trade purposes.

The English authorities were not entirely asleep, and when William Burnet became Governor of New York and New Jersey (April 19, 1720), by royal appointment, he came to New York, where he found talk about Niagara of such moment that, within a month after his arrival, he dispatched a message to the Lords of Trade proposing to fortify the frontier to prevent the French "from seducing the Senecas". He then entered into a lively correspondence with the Governor of Canada. The French were spurred to build a stone fort at Niagara, which the English attacked by indirection by building a fortification and trading post at Oswego. The French built so well that one of their buildings, "The House of Peace," still stands on the old site. Its walls are thick, but it has no appearance of being a fort, hence the name, expressing its hoped-for intentions, though it was surrounded by a palisade and had a guard house. Apparently the French had scored a great victory, but we must look toward Albany for the English counterattack. If the Gaul fought one way, the Saxon fought another way.

6. The English Awaken.

The Albany Council. Governor Burnet convoked a council at Albany in September, 1726, and in careful explanation of the situation, pointed out that the presence of a French fort was decidedly contrary to the interests of the Iroquois. He also exacted from the Onondaga representatives the admission that *all the Niagara land belonged to the Seneca, including the adjacent land across the river.* So adroitly did Burnet present the case, that he placed the Indians in the position of being the wronged parties, who should lodge vigorous complaints, and then offered the help of the English authorities. He followed up this advantage by persuading them to ratify the deed of 1701, and then to deed to the English all the hunting grounds south of Lake Ontario and reaching the Niagara river, in all, a strip sixty miles wide. By this strategy the French fort on the Niagara now lay on English soil. This, however, did not mean that the French were going to evacuate at once; it merely meant that the English had a paper right to eject them if they could do so by force on the pretext of ownership. A full generation intervened before this coup was accomplished. The elder Joncaire died at Niagara, June 29, 1739,—the year that Chautauqua lake was discovered. Joncaire had a large family of boys, two of whom remained in the wilderness to carry out their father's work. These young men were the principal reliance of New France, and the opponents of a new figure who rose to advance the British interests in New York—William Johnson, a young Irishman.

Irondequoit and Oswego. The next move of the awakening English was to acquire a tract of land on Irondequoit bay. This tract, twenty by thirty miles in extent, was purchased on January 10, 1740, but was not settled, it being deemed an inexpedient time. Governor Clarke of New York, who was an important agent in developing English interests along the Ontario shores, saw the pressing need of a strong position on the Irondequoit. Later Governor Clinton urged this same proposal, and in 1749 William Johnson wrote Clinton urging settlement there as a means of attracting the Indians and shutting out the French who were trying to buy a tract in this locality. The English and the Dutch settlers somehow lacked the verve and vision of the French and, more than this, they lacked the capacity for establishing cordial relations with the

Indians. The pusillanimous flight of the English traders from Oswego, for fear of a massacre, at the very time when the Indians were paddling into the bay with canoe loads of peltries, stands out in significant contrast to the courage and determination of the French, in their isolated positions, under circumstances even more trying. The Indians, naturally, were a bit disgusted with the English, espcially as they had to turn back once more and trade with the French (1744), who, of course, received them with loud acclaims and flattering expressions of comradeship.

7. William Johnson Becomes a Factor.

William Johnson. We have already mentioned William Johnson. As Joncaire, the elder, was to the French, so William Johnson was destined to be to the English. In his British ability and Celtic personality rested the fate of English hopes west of the Mohawk. He came to America from Ireland, being the son of Christopher Johnson and Anne Warren. He was educated as a barrister, but just before his examination, his uncle, Admiral Sir Peter Warren, offered him an opportunity to sail with him to America, where, under royal grant, he had a tract of land on the Mohawk river. The adventure appealed to this young man of 22 years, and he accepted with eagerness the post of chief steward of Sir Peter's lands. Young Johnson landed in New York city in December, 1737, and spent the winter there, leaving in the Spring in a sloop laden with mill supplies. The settlement of Warrensbush on the Mohawk was soon laid out, and here young William showed his acumen. His uncle had hoped to preserve his grant intact and to rent or lease parts of it to the Dutch, German and Scotch settlers, but tenancy was something of which these people had had enough in the old world. Young William advised the outright sale of the property in farmstead lots. This move attracted real settlers willing to risk all on the success of their own property and to defend it against all invaders. It was the building of "the American ideal".

During his sojourn along the river, young Johnson had an abundant opportunity to study the Indians who came to visit the settlers and traders. He mingled with the Mohawk, learned their language, took part in their ceremonies, and in many other ways demonstrated a sympathy and understanding that was rare enough for a phlegmatic Britisher. He soon discovered that the policy and management of the Board of Colonial Commissioners with relation to Indian trade was lax and criminal. Indian traders of any class and without regard to character were licensed for an inconsiderable fee. Thus the Indians were subjected to many frauds and indignities that greatly prejudiced them against the English. William Johnson kept up a vigorous and voluminous correspondence on this subject with Governor George Clinton, and so commended himself for his business ability that he was soon placed in British service as Superintendent of Indian Affairs. This was a most fortunate thing for the Six Nations. It was even more so for the English colonists.

Investment of Canada. By 1747 it was decided by the colonists that Canada should be invested. William Johnson was commissioned Colonel and second in command under Sir William Peppernell. The Five Nations agreed to furnish one thousand warriors, the Seneca promising reliable aid. Little was done, however, except to hold the frontier against French invasion, for the Treaty of Aix-la-Chappelle brought an armistice. Seven years later the battle of Lake George was fought resulting in the defeat of Dieskau. In this engagement Johnson fought with such ability that he was rewarded by a gift from Parliament of five thousand pounds sterling and the King dubbed him a baronet. This recognition was not only because Johnson had shown unusual military ability, but because he had held allegiance of the Indian nations. The Iroquois had visible proof that it was expedient, at least, to cling to the British. The Seneca yielded Niagara to the will of the English, and all the Iroquois was agreed to take the field against the French. This caused the result of Johnson's council at Canajoharie in April, 1759. Events now followed fast. Niagara* was stormed and taken, the French capitulating to Sir William Johnson. It was a glowing victory, the result of long preparation, and a fulfillment of the logic destiny.

The Fall of Niagara. The victory of Niagara had been anticipated by Sir William the year before in his report to the Board of Trade. He was confident, he said, that he could lead against the French, not only the Five Nations of the Iroquois, but also many of the Indians who had been particularly under the domination of the French at LaGalette. It is thus seen that, through the influence of Johnson, even the Genesee Seneca were ready to war against their old friends, whom Joncaire had cemented to them by many ties of allegiance and even blood, for the French had intermarried to a considerable extent in some of the Seneca villages. It was good evidence that good faith and square dealing were more effective than even a "hail fellow well met policy".

Niagara capitulated, and as Sir William entered the fort, he found a host of English captives there to rejoice with him. He also met the two sons of Joncaire, Thomas and Daniel. General Amherst who had planned the attack, was in the north, where Ticonderoga and Crown

---

*The story of the siege of Niagara is nowhere better told than by Dr. Frank H. Severance in his "Old Frontier of France".

Point soon fell, Quebec following on September 18th. Two years later Lord Amherst, rallying his troops from Oswego, fell upon Montreal, which capitulated. Canada was now in English hands, thanks to Johnson and his Iroquois allies.

It must be noted that Sir William was not originally in command at the Niagara siege, but that his superior officer was General John Prideaux, who was killed. This left the forces in Colonel Johnson's command and he made the most of his responsibility.

8. The Conspiracy of Pontiac.

Pontiac. If the fall of Canada had a profound effect upon the Indians, it had a still more far reaching effect upon the destiny and direction of English civilization and control in North America. It meant that France should go no further, and that England should now expand in lines the nature of which one could only vaguely dream. The fall of New France, however, did not solve the problems of the border, though it aroused the Indians to a realization of England's power and determination. In the west, the Indians were therefore troubled with the thought that the English would extend their domain so far that the tribes of red men would be driven into the sunset sea, a fear that was indeed prophetic.

To crystallize these fears, Pontiac, chief of the Ottawa, arose to preach that the Indians must regain their rights and independence and that they must return to the ways of their fathers. He gathered together a confederacy of tribes, and with sudden attack took all the western strongholds save Detroit. Overtures had been secretly made to the Iroquois and all but a portion of the Seneca-Huron descendants rejected participation in the conspiracy and reported the hostile activities in the west to their English allies.

Plate 15. Cornplanter (Gyantwaka) or John Abeal. He was the son of a Dutch trader of Albany and an Indian mother. For many years he was an able leader of the Seneca people, and frequently cooled the hasty temper of his contemporary, Red Jacket. He left numerous descendants under the names of Cornplanter and Obail. While living at Kanadesaga (Geneva) in 1756, he had a white wife and several children.

The Genesee-Seneca Conspire to Involve Their Nation. The Chippewa, Ottawa, Wyandot, Pottawatomie, Delaware, Mingoe, Shawnee, and many other tribes were united to execute Pontiac's ingenious conspiracy. No other Indian leader had ever brought together so many tribes for a single purpose. If the Six Nations of the Iroquois had given their assent to the proposition, there can be no doubt that New York would have suffered severely. As it was, the Genesee-Seneca (naturalized Huron) were secretly attempting to join Pontiac, and their young warriors had sent wampum belts to the northwest tribes, inviting an attack on Niagara, and then Fort Pitt. Johnson heard of the proposal, and acted.

He set out with a retinue for Detroit, stopping at Niagara, where he called a council of the Seneca. He charged them with the plot, and one of their spokesmen, Huron-like, indignantly denied it, putting on the air of injured innocence. Sir William, who generally spoke with gracious urbanity, now thundered his denunciations, and demanded that the Seneca send a deputation of chiefs to Detroit, to repeat before the assembled Indian tribes their innocence and disapprobation of the proposals of the Seneca messengers, who had borne their villainous proposals to the supporters of Pontiac, attested by wampum belts. Sir William then contemptuously threw back the wampum belt that had been given him with the suave speech denying guilt. This meant that he would not yet believe the Seneca statement. After consultation, they agreed to send delegates to Detroit, bearing belts as testimony that the nation spoke. The Senecaized Huron were thus compelled to swallow their own poison, and make the best of it.

The Detroit Council. Johnson and his party reached Detroit, and with the firing of two cannon convoked the great council. From far and near, they had come to see, more than to discuss, for the magic of Sir William's name was a marvelous thing to the nations of the west. Here was a white man who had made his great stone house the council hall of a mighty confederacy, a man who sometimes lived as an Indian and who fearlessly thundered the truth. Johnson and his officers appeared in full uniform; the Indian chiefs were in their paint and feathers. Sir William made a friendly address, earnest though lengthy and explicit. The next day Indian delegates from the northwest made acceptable replies. Then arose Kaiaghshota, chief of the Genesee-Seneca, and with studied oratory and eloquence disingenuously disclaimed all connection with the plot and absolved his nation from guilt. To the surprise of the assemblage, Adiaraghta, the Wyandot, sprang to his feet and accused the Seneca of duplicity, pointing out exactly how he had been one of the chief conspirators, and one of the ambassadors who had brought the war belts and proposals of Seneca participation. White Mingo, an Ohio Indian, then arose and accused the Wyandot himself of being a conspirator and a principal in inciting his own people. Excitement ran high and a fight was imminent. Sir William, with the details of the plot revealed, quickly dissolved the council. He returned to his home in the Mohawk valley and cultivated the good will of the Iroquois, who at all cost should be kept from evil alliance. His success was complete, to the disappointment of the Ottawa who vowed to take his life.

The Seneca Nation Exonerated. The Genesee-Seneca, as we have observed, were unfriendly for two principal reasons: First, they were the descendants of the broken Canadian tribes and the adopted nations of the south; they had been under the domination of the French so long that their sympathies were naturally estranged from the English. Their equivocal speeches

were not without some justification, as Sir William
knew. The official councils of the Seneca had never
entered into any conspiracy but had always cautioned
peace. Thus the Seneca officially were not guilty. The
guilt lay with the young warriors who, against the will
of the civil chiefs, had taken the tomahawk in their own
hands and gone over to the enemy. It was the guilt of
individuals in concert and not the guilt of the nation as
an organized entity. Johnson afterward wisely plead
this in a reply to Amherst, as only a student of Iroquois
government could do it.

9. The Tragedy at Devil's Hole.

Seneca Claims on the Niagara. The Seneca had
yet another grievance that was gnawing at their vitals.
It was the suspicion that the English had actually construed their deeds and beaver-land cessions as an outright surrender of ownership. To the Indian way of
thinking this was an error, for it is presumable that they
meant to convey only the *limited right of occupation* in
return for which they were to receive protection. This
must be kept in mind, for it is the explanation for a
bloody event that followed. It will be remembered that
the Seneca believed that they owned the land on the
Niagara along which lay the portage road and the
carrying place around the rapids and the falls. This
portage road had been built by the English under Sir
William and terminated at Fort Schlosser above the
cataract. It followed the banks of the river above the
terrifying cliffs, and three miles from the falls passed
a deep ravine with precipitous walls and jagged crags
below. The place was called Devil's Hole.

Devil's Hole. Here, on the 14th of September,
1763, a tragedy was destined to occur. A small convoy
of twenty-four men under a sergeant, returning from
the discharge of goods at Fort Niagara, marched along

the road until they came to Devil's Hole. At this point they were surprised by an irregular body of five hundred Seneca Indians, who had lain in ambush awaiting their coming. Rushing forth, they overwhelmed the party with musket fire and then scalped their victims. The militia at the fort, hearing firing, hurried out to render assistance and, though they were two companies strong, they also were ambushed, killed or driven over the precipice. Only three escaped,—one a drummer boy, who was caught by the limb of a projecting tree, and one an officer who escaped on his horse, while bullets rained around him.

The Seneca were not after booty, and did not loot the wagon train or the dead. They simply wanted to terrify the English and cause an abandonment of Niagara. Their act was one designed to emphasize their ownership of the land and to prove their right to resist trespass.

This stroke lent comfort to the western allies of Pontiac, but the Iroquois as a body repudiated it as an official act, and the Mohawk repledged their loyalty to Sir William, using all their influence to hold their comrades in check, and to keep the young men from rushing to aid in the western movements of Pontiac's bands.

10. Lord Amherst's Threat.

Pontiac Submits. Pontiac, defeated at every turn, soon sued for peace and sent his pipe to Sir William in testimony of his desire to submit. His rebellion had been crushed and many of his bravest men killed in the operations of Bouquet and Amherst. Amherst was willing to forgive the Canadian Indians, but was bitter against the Seneca, whom he thought should be wiped off the face of the earth. Indeed, he formulated a plan to enlist ten thousand men and add them to an army of eleven thousand British regulars, who should scour the country and kill every Seneca male, the women being distributed to the other tribes. The plan was well conceived and was a feasible one. If Amherst could have proceeded, the Seneca would have been completely wiped out. One thing stood in thé way of its operation; Sir William Johnson objected. He explained that the Seneca nation as such was not at fault.

The Seneca Surrender Their Conspirators. Amherst's plan, however, was not without its fruit. The Seneca heard of it and, seeing its terrible possibilities, immediately began to make overtures for a genuine peace. They were humble indeed in their pleas and promises. Amherst then demanded that they surrender the chief offenders and "instigators" of the plots against the English. The Seneca did this with surprising alacrity, turning over nineteen culprits. Of these two were publicly hanged at Onondaga, and the rest imprisoned in New York. This was a more frightful revenge than open war in the minds of the Seneca and they were deeply impressed. Pontiac surrendered in 1766, and fortunately for the Indians, General Amherst, three years before had become Governor of Virginia. This left the Seneca in the hands of Sir William, and he had little difficulty in showing them where their interests lay.

11. The Beginning of Metes and Bounds.

The Niagara Council. Sir William met Pontiac at Oswego, where he smoked the pipe of peace with him and received his oath of allegiance to the King of England. Sir William now proceeded to Niagara, where he held a council with every Indian tribe that had any relations with the French or with the conspiracy. The peace here secured endured until the outbreak of another war, a war of far reaching consequences. It was not to be an Indian war, but a revolt of the colonists against their own King. In the meantime the Iroquois Indians, as well as many other tribes, were linked by increasing ties of trade and contact with the English, and soon looked upon King George as their "great father over the seas". Through all of the difficulties in which Sir William found himself, he had the loyal aid of Joseph Brant, a war chief of the Mohawk, whose sister Molly was his housekeeper and, after Indian customs, his wife. The combination of Johnson and Brant was a rare one and far-reaching in its beneficial consequences. It meant that Johnson could speak and that the Iroquois could understand.

Joseph Brant. It would be of great interest to follow at considerable length the career of Joseph Brant, for, though not a resident of the Genesee country, he had a large share in shaping its destiny and in influencing the course of the Seneca. Though a Mohawk of the Mohawks, Joseph Brant was born in an Indian settlement on the Ohio in 1742. His native name was Thayendadegea. After the death of his father, a Canojoharie Mohawk, his mother returned to her homeland, bringing with her Joseph and his sister Molly. Thereafter, both sister and brother were destined to a life of movement and adventure. Joseph was "discovered" by Sir William and sent to an Indian mission school maintained by Doctor Whelock. Here, he studied with unusual diligence for two years and, in 1763, returned to the Mohawk valley, where he entered the service of Sir William at an unusually good salary. His ability as a leader among his own people was immediately evident, and Johnson found him an invaluable aid, whose loyalty and judgment could be relied upon. These qualities were indeed most important at a time when the Indians were feeling dissatisfied with the attitude of the settlers. Seneca Indians and others were being murdered by border ruffians, and the Seneca were fast losing patience. They feared not only extermination by the settlers but the complete loss of their lands. The apprehension was quite general. It became necessary that a boundary line be definitely fixed.

The Fort Stanwix Council. The work of arranging a council by which the line between the whites and the Indians should be fixed fell naturally upon Sir William, who decided that it should be held at the great portage upon which Fort Stanwix stood. An abundance of provisions was sent on from Albany, at Johnson's request. The council, held in October, 1768, opened with the presence of more than three thousand Indian delegates from the Six Nations and their dependent tribes, the Shawnee, Delaware and Ohio Seneca. Many important colonial officials attended the conference, among them the Governors of Pennsylvania and New Jersey. The boundary line was determined and a term of sale agreed upon for all the land claimed by the English. For this land the sum of $50,000 was to be turned over to the Indians, a sum that the King of England felt was too great to give mere natives, but little did he know them, or that they had discovered a use for silver (see Fig. 10).

The New Boundary. The boundary line started at a point on Wood creek, not far from Fort Stanwix, and ran south-east to the forks of the Unadilla river, then along the Unadilla to its junction with the Susquehanna; thence south to the bend of the Delaware (at the present location of Deposit); thence south-east along the Delaware a few miles below the site of Hancock; thence north-westward to a point below Owego; thence along the Susquehanna to the mouth of Towanda creek; thence in a direct air line to a point at the confluence of the Monongahela and the Alleghany. All the land to the east of this line was to be ceded to the King, and both he and his subjects were to recognize all land

to the west of this line as Six Nations' domain.   The
exceptions were certain reservations about the Mohawk
villages.

12.   The Savagery of the Border Whites.

There were many objections on the part of the
Indians and the settlers to certain portions of this line

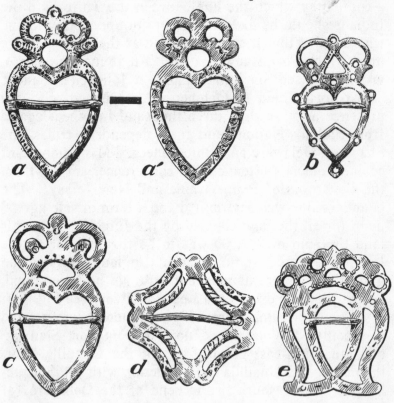

H.B.

Fig. 10. Iroquois brooches of silver copied from Scotch "Lucken-
booth" brooches. The Indians flattened silver coins and cut brooches
from them by the thousands. a-a'. Scotch brooch and reverse.
b. Scotch brooch. c. d. e. Seneca brooches.

and, though the Indians had the utmost confidence in
Sir William, they had no such confidence in certain
settlers and traders, who sought at every opportunity
to defraud them and to kill their people.   The line was

Plate 16. William Tallchief. A Seneca of the Cattaraugus reservation. Born c. 1858, died 1918. His ancestors were captive Shawnee.

designed to keep each party from encroaching upon the other, but the Seneca knew only too well that no English settler would stay on his own side of the fence if he saw an acre or a pelt on the Indian's side.

White Savages. Scarcely six months passed before Sir William found it again necessary to make a journey to the Onondaga, the Cayuga and the Seneca, for the purpose of getting full particulars relating to the outrages of the settlers committed upon Six Nations people. His objective was the town of Kanadesaga (near Geneva), where he had summoned the Ohio Seneca to met with him and their brethren. Sir William was well received by his Indian friends, who poured into his ear a long list of grievances, and showed how innumerable frauds had been practiced upon them. The sympathy of Sir William was all with them and he returned to his Mohawk valley home full of indignation. Indeed, in his report to the Earl of Hillsborough, he said that even on his journey home he was overtaken with the news of the murder of an inoffensive Seneca lad, who was fired upon by some frontiersman on the Susquehanna. The murder was all the more inexcusable since the father of the youth and his whole family were zealous partisans of the English settlers. It was not the only murder, for many others were recited by Johnson in his statement. He also mentions a murderous attack upon Callendar, a trader on his way to Fort Pitt with twenty-five horses laden with Indian trader articles. The assailants were *thirty white men disguised as Indians.* The Earl of Hillsborough carried the complaint to the King, who, in turn, wrote to his colonial governors asking them to take steps to prevent this violence and encroachment.

Indians Murdered. Contrary to the order of the King, trouble continued and Indians were murdered by settlers at every opportunity, until Indian patience was exhausted. Johnson well knew that the Indians did not begin reprisals until all other methods had seemingly failed. He did his best to calm the Indians and to prevent the settlers from murdering them, and in his letter to Earl Dartmouth he expresses his difficulty. "My negotiations," he wrote, "with the Senecas were interrupted by intelligence that a certain Mr. Cressop, an inhabitant of Virginia, had murdered forty Indians on the Oho, for the most part of the Six Nations."

Indeed, so savage were these border ruffians that they murdered Indian women and killed their children, and even scalped them. The old and friendly did not escape, for even the kindly old Bald Eagle, chief of the Delaware, a man who had mingled with the whites for many years, was murdered in his canoe while on his way down the Kanhawa. Tearing the scalp from the old man's head, his murderer set his body upright and set the canoe again adrift down the stream.* The favorite chief of the Shawnee met a similar fate. Old Silver Heels, the chief, had undertaken in the kindest manner to guide a party of white traders through the forest from the Ohio country to Albany, and was murdered enroute.

13. Cresap's War.

The Indians Resist. The bloody raids of the settlers continued until the Indians could no longer endure them in silence, and *Cresap's war* followed. Prominent in the Indian forces were Logan, the Mingo chief, and Chief Cornstalk. Indian raids began with fatal success, and in all of them the humanity of Logan was conspicuous, so much so that, in spite of the fact that his wife and children had been murdered, the Indians called him, "the white man's friend". At length

*For these and other instances, see Ketchum's Buffalo and the Senecas, Vol. 1, pages 162 to 165 ff.

the Virginia bordermen mustered their regiments and a battle was fought at the mouth of the Kanhawa. It was one of the most sanguinary, considering the number of combatants, in the history of colonial encounters. The Indians eventually retreated after being surrounded, but the losses they inflicted were too heavy to justify their opponents' claim as victors.

Logan. Peace was sought by Lord Dunsmore, and a messenger was dispatched to the cabin of Logan. It was upon this occasion that Logan made his celebrated speech, counted as one of the master-pieces of tragic eloquence. Colonel John Gibson, with his officers, came into the Indian village, and saw Logan and Cornstalk. The former invited the officers to walk out a little ways with him. Then, with his face bathed in tears and exhibiting every evidence of deep anguish, Logan spoke. He said:

"I appeal to any white man to say if he ever entered Logan's cabin hungry and he gave him not meat; if he ever came cold and naked and he warmed him not. During the course of the last long bloody war, Logan remained idle in his cabin, an advocate of peace. Such was my love for the whites that my countrymen pointed as they passed, and said, 'Logan is the friend of the white man.' I had thought to live with you, but for the injuries of one man. Colonel Cresap, the last spring, in cold blood and unprovoked, murdered all the relatives of Logan; not even sparing my women and children. There runs not a drop of my blood in the veins of any living creature. This called on me for revenge; I have sought it; I have killed many; I have fully glutted my revenge. For my country, I rejoice at the beams of peace, but do not harbor the thought that mine is the joy of fear. Logan never felt fear. He will not turn on his heel to save his life. Who is there to mourn for Logan? Not one!"

14. Kanadesaga or Old Castle.

In considering the part taken by the Seneca and their confederates against the colonists in the events that follow, we must keep in mind their smouldering resentment against the settlers and their love and loyalty to Sir William Johnson and the royal power that he represented. It must be considered, however, that many of the Indians had a happier experience with the settlers, and that missionary influence, particularly that of Rev. Samuel Kirkland among the Oneida and Tuscarora, was of a kind that cemented them to their white neighbors. His influence and activities were mostly confined to these people, though he had sojourned among the Seneca in 1764 and 1766, having during his visitation kept a journal which is of large importance today. It is one of our best sources of information concerning the life in the great Seneca town of Kanadesaga (though the description of "The Old Castle," as it was called, by Ezra Buel is excellent also).

Old Castle. It was in Kanadesaga that Sayenquerhaghta, "the Old King," dwelt. He was the leading chief of the Seneca and greatly respected by them. When Kirkland came to the Old Castle (or Seneca Castle, Kanadesaga), he was received by Old King (also called Old Smoke, Disappearing Smoke and Sayenqueraghta), and given protection by him even to the extent of an adoption.

In the midst of a rugged forest clearing two miles long and a mile wide, Old Castle had its nestling place. In its center was a block-house with a roof well protected by a parapet and a spacious stockade surrounding its grounds. East and west from this imposing symbol of strength ran the Broadway of the "castle," full one hundred fifty feet wide. Along this highway on either side were the log houses of the Seneca. They were widely spaced, for each house had its own yard and garden, but the average lot was not more than two hundred feet wide, though some were closer together. The log houses were comfortable enough, having stoned-up fire places, swinging cranes and the usual pots and kettles always found in the homes of the settlers. There were even Dutch ovens and roasting spits, pans and skillets. The best homes had floors of split logs smoothed off and neatly fitted, but the more humble cabins had floors of beaten clay. For rugs they had pelts of bear, deer and elk skin, and often mats of woven rushes. Ezra Buel, who went with the English surveying party in 1765, left an interesting account of Old Castle, and in it exclaims, "Altogether the Seneca at Old Castle live as well as most of the white settlers in a new country".

15. Seneca Life, 1755-1775.

Tribal Conditions. The Seneca of this period tilled the land in common, after their ancient practices, and had communal store houses. Their crops were corn, beans, squashes, pumpkins and melons; while from their orchards they picked apples, pears, plums and peaches. They had little need for cows, for the woods about them furnished plenty of meat. Horses were preferred as domestic animals, as they were more easily cared for, and could forage for themselves in winter, if encouraged with a daily supply of corn.

The Seneca of Old Castle in 1765 dressed for the most part like white people of the frontier. Their own native "cuts" were still to be observed, and, even when flannel and broadcloth were employed, they used the Indian style of hunting shirt. Leather leggings were the vogue and moccasins were the common foot gear. Some

*See Buel, A. C., "Sir William Johnson," p. 237. ff.

of the Indians here treasured military coats, which they
donned on ceremonial occasions.   The women were

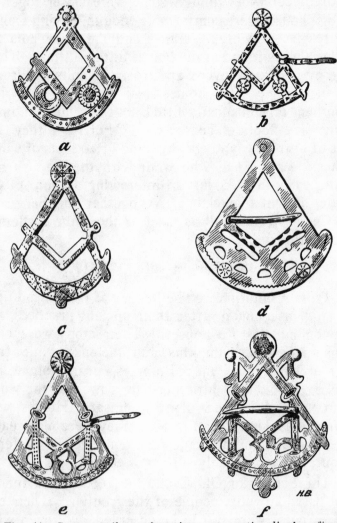

Fig. 11. Seneca silver brooches conventionalized after the
Masonic emblems worn by Sir William Johnson and Joseph Brant. The
Iroquois were very fond of this pattern.

neatly dressed in broadcloth skirts, flannel underskirts
and leggings.   Their overdresses were often of light
flannel or turkey-cloth of solid color, green, red or blue,

and profusely beaded.   Ribbons were neatly sewed on
around the collar and bottom, and row after row of
silver brooches ornamented the clothing of those who
had wealth and position.

East of the Seneca town was the trading post on
the lake shore.   Here lived the traders, the British
representative and the gunsmith, together with their
clerks and their families.   It was a busy place, for here
the Indians from near and far transacted their business,
and here stopped many of the travelers, traders and messengers on their way to distant tribes and posts.

Some of the Indians of Old Castle were well versed
in the ways of the English settlers, and the trader had
as clerks two Indian boys who had been educated at
Canajoharie.   The old chief, Sayenqueraghta, though
unlettered, was a man of extraordinary intelligence and
judgment, and from his council house governed his
people with great ability.   His humane qualities and
sympathy for human suffering are remarked by Kirkland.   Old Castle was far from being a town of mere
savages, and this picture has been extended that we
might catch a vision of the kind of people who were
attached to the British at the outbreak of the Revolutionary war.   Old Castle was destined to see troubled
times, the reason for which we shall shortly describe.

16.   The Revolt of the Colonists against the King.

Indian Perplexity.   The Seneca had little knowledge that the colonists were gradually becoming irri-
tated at the action of Crown agents, or that a steady
resistance was being developed.   They only knew that
Sir William Johnson and his deputies continually urged
them to cling to their loyalty to England.   This was not
difficult, for the Indians found the colonists oftentimes
their antagonists, while the agents of the Crown interposed to protect them.   Settlers murdered Indians, but
the agents of the King gave them presents of food,

clothing and utensils.   Whom then should they trust?
Should it be Sir William, Brant and the loyal subjects
of the Crown to whom they had pledged allegiance and
support?   Or should they believe the complaints of
Herkimer, Kirkland and Philip Schuyler, for all of whom
they also had a high regard?   The Seneca were greatly
perplexed, but wished to remain neutral,—at least this
was their first feeling.

Johnson's Death.   During July, 1774, a large body
of Indians congregated at Johnson Hall to seek Sir William's advice and interposition in the Ohio war led by
Lord Dunmore.   The 11th of July was a hot and dis-
agreeable day, and Sir William had been sick for several
days, yet for two hours he addressed his Indian friends.
After this effort he collapsed, and two hours later
breathed into the ears of his brother-in-law, Joseph
Brant, these words: "Joseph, control your people, control
your people! I am going away." His last efforts were in
behalf of the Indian race.

Thus, amid a great concourse of his Indian friends,
the spirit of Sir William passed out.   Word quickly
spread that Colonel Johnson's last words were spoken
in the Iroquois tongue and that he had passed on his
authority to Joseph Brant.   Soon afterward Brant was
elected the grand military chief of the Six Nations, and
many Indians believed that Sir William's power had
descended to one of their own blood and kin.   What
effect this belief had upon them we have yet to see.   As
a matter of fact, the succession in office as British
Superintendent fell to Colonel Guy Johnson, upon
whose shoulders now rested a dangerous and impossible
task.

Problems of the Revolution.   There could be no
doubt that the colonists were arming for a conflict with
the Crown, and Sir William had debated this subject
with gloomy forebodings before he died.   By April,

Plate 17. Delos Big Kettle (Sai-no-wah). Big Kettle, of the Wolf Clan, Cattaraugus Seneca, was one of the able leaders of the non-Christian party. Born c. 1861, died 1923.

Plate 18. Mrs. John Big Kettle, of the Wolf Clan. Cattaraugus Seneca, and mother of Delos Big Kettle. The Big Kettles were descended from the Seneca who once lived in the vicinity of Mount Morris. Born c. 1822, died 1923.

1775, when the news of Lexington reached Johnson Hall, it was clearly seen that the colonists were ready to resist the King and his red coats. Tory and colonist alike saw that the Six Nations were to be reckoned with. The British held out every inducement, and not only promised the Indians great benefits from this war, but urged them to preserve their alliance with the Crown and to punish the rebellious subjects who made war. The patriots sought to explain the reason for their rebellion, that the Six Nations might understand their cause, but the reasons were beyond their comprehension, and Christianized Indians replied to their missionary teachers, "You taught us to be loyal to the King, and all our prayers ended with a petition that God save him."

Iroquois Desire Neutrality. The Six Nations did not act upon the importunities of the Crown, but, with the possible exception of the Mohawk, desired to hold aloof. The Oneida, Tuscarora* and river Mohikan and Stockbridge declared their intention to support their friends among the settlers, and thus alienated themselves from the sympathy of Brant. Thus was the famous Iroquois Confederacy divided by the most serious difference that had affected it since its inception.

Even the Seneca, though they desired to remain neutral for the most part, were not united in their loyalty to the British, but a division of them headed by Big Tree, an amiable Genesee chief of much influence, strongly favored the colonies and worked actively for them. The Seneca at this time were peacefully pursuing their farming and hunting, having found satisfaction in the arts of peace. Mary Jemison in her narrative relates that "for twelve or fifteen years (after the French War) the use of implements of war was not known, nor the war whoop heard, save on days of festivity, when the achievements of former days were

---

*The Tuscarora became the sixth nation in 1722.

commemorated in a kind of mimic warfare". In the seventh chapter of Mary Jemison's story we find an excellent picture of the period just before the outbreak of the American Revolution.

17. The Battle of Oriskany.

Fort Stanwix. To create a favorable impression, as allies of the British the Seneca were invited with their tribal brothers to witness the battle at the taking of Fort Stanwix. It was an invitation to witness a holiday party, in which the colonists should be whipped by the well-drilled and handsomely dressed British militia. This would impress the Iroquois with the power of the British and the expediency of supporting them against the rebellious settlers! All that the Indians were asked to do was "to sit down, smoke their pipes and look on," said Mary Jemison. She continued her account by saying that, "Contrary to expectations, instead of smoking and looking on, they were obliged to fight for their lives; and in the end of the battle were completely beaten, with a great loss in killed and wounded. Our Indians alone had thirty-six killed and a great number wounded." Such was the participation of the Seneca in the first real battle, that of Oriskany, *the place of nettles*.

Herkimer's Victory. The Tory forces were under the command of St. Leger and the Indians were under Brant. The opposing colonists were under General Herkimer. Arrayed against him besides the regulars and the Indians, were the Rangers under Colonel Butler. The British forces were on their way to Fort Stanwix, which the patriots had rechristened Fort Schuyler, when Herkimer with forces cautiously approached with a body of eight hundred to one thousand men. Herkimer knew something of border warfare and his extreme caution displeased some of his younger officers who urged an immediate advance. Unfortunately he yielded and fell into an ambuscade in an unfavorable place. The fight was precipitous and wild disorder ensued before the General could bring about an order of battle. Stone in his "Buffalo and the Senecas" has described the battle of Oriskany with great vividness, and ends by saying, "— the Indians perceiving with what ardor the Provincials maintained the fight, and finding their own numbers sadly diminished, now raised the retreating cry of 'Oonah' and fled in every direction". With the flight of the Indians, the British Greens and Rangers began a retreat toward the fort where firing indicated that their presence was needed. Even here the patriots were successful in driving away John Johnson and in putting the Indians to flight.

This battle, though an accident of war, was a happy omen. For the first time the Stars and Stripes had floated over an American force in battle, and under it Americans had withstood the baptism of fire. Here under its sacred folds Americans had poured forth their blood that America might be free.

Old King Takes Command. The nettles of Oriskany left irritating burns upon the breasts of the Seneca, and scars that would not heal. Chiefs who advised peace were scorned, and even Molly Brant, with tears and every display of strong emotion, urged the Seneca to follow their English allies. She scored the peaceful and venerable Sayenqueraghta, and reminded him of his friendship for Sir William. This appeal by the widow of the great Johnson was not without fruit, for it served to arouse the Seneca to action. The Old King of Old Castle now resolved to lead forth his men to war for the friend now dead who had been a friend of the King.

18. Cherry Valley and Wyoming.

Massacres. The work of Brant was indefatigable and when the Seneca finally became active partisans, they were put to their bloody work under Tory orders at Cherry Valley. Later they descended upon Wyoming, in the Susquehanna Valley, and by an adroit movement came upon the settlement at a time when the militia was watching for them in another direction. Brant was not present but a leader equally able commanded the Seneca; he was Sayenqueraghta.

Once the Colonial forces at Wyoming surrendered, no lives were taken, but during the battle the carnage was frightful. Many of the Seneca reverted to their primitive savagery and wallowed in blood and reeked with scalps still warm. It must be said, however, in justice to them, that no women or children were killed by direct attack. Smarting as they were from their former defeat, the Seneca at Wyoming had full opportunity to glut their revenge, and yet the restraint that they showed is no less than remarkable. Every historian knows that this battle might have been a massacre indeed, had the Seneca so willed it. They had not forgotten the murder of their own women and children.

Once the young warriors had experienced the intoxication of war they thirsted for other campaigns. British agents and officers among them incited them to revenge and argued that the Seneca must remain loyal to the King. But all the Seneca were not agreed to this, among them Chief Big Tree*, who in 1778 had spent some time with General Washington. During the summer Washington sent the Chief among his people to urge them to take the side of the colonies. Big Tree was successful in a measure among certain groups but a spy spread the news through Old Castle (Genundasega) and Genesee Castle (Little Beard's Town, Dyu-non-da-ga-geh) that the Americans were preparing to invade the land of the Seneca and drive them out. Whether

---
*Big Tree's Seneca name was Ga-on-do-go-wa.

the rumor had basis or not at the time, it was a shrewd guess at what was actually to happen a few months later. Big Tree could no longer prevail upon his people, whose villages were filled with warriors from far distant settlements. If they had formerly been inclined to peace they were now for war with those who fought to invade their land.

19. A Glimpse at the Seneca Villages.

At this period there were no palisaded Seneca villages. All were laid out on open ground with fields about them. No longer did the bark lodge predominate, for now houses were built of logs and even boards. Some houses were of neat appearances and well painted, their surroundings showing evidence of thrift and real taste. The Seneca felt themselves secure, and had it not been for the white man's war they would have been happy indeed.

Old Castle. The great town of Old Castle contained fifty comfortable houses and was surrounded by flourishing fields and orchards; further west was Kanandaigua, a town of twenty-three houses, situated a mile from the lake on the west side. The houses here were large and comfortable, having well-built fire places. There were those who remarked that it resembled in appearance a little settlment of white settlers. Further west near the foot of Honeoye lake was the village of Hanneyaye, a hamlet of from fifteen to twenty cabins, and all about it were fine fields and flourishing orchards.

Seneca Towns. The Genesee-Seneca had numerous little villages and several large towns. The largest was Little Beard's Town, a settlement of one hundred and twenty-eight houses. Canawagus, on the west side of the Genesee opposite Avon, was regarded as a place where the trails converged. Ganosgago was at Dansville, Dyuneganooh at Caledonia, Ohagi near Leicester,

Onundaoh near Nunda, Deyuitgoah at Squawkie Hill, Gahnyuhsas near the outlet of Conesus lake, Big Kettle's town near Mount Morris, Gawshegweoh near Williamburg, Ganundase at Moscow, Deowesta at Portageville, Gahnagadot at East Avon, Sgahisga-ah at Lima and Gaondowanuh, Big Tree, in Leicester on the west side of the river. Besides these there were several smaller settlements and clusters of cabins. There was a village at Naples and several along the Susquehanna trail, particularly a large and fine settlement at Newtown, near Elmira, where the Seneca had colonized their Sauk captives from their western wars, while Catherinestown was just south of Seneca lake. To the west along the Tonawanda trail were settlements at Tonawanda (town of Alabama), and along the Cattaraugus and the Alleghany were several thriving villages little known to history.

20. Sullivan's Campaign.

Sullivan Strikes. The young Indian braves along the frontier, influenced by the British, began to fall upon outlying settlements, and render other aid to the red coats, until the wrath of the colonial government could no longer be withheld. General Washington planned to have General Gates attack the Seneca in their own territory, but Gates refused, upon which the command of the projected expedition devolved upon General John Sullivan, a New Hampshire lawyer of distinction. His orders were to invade the Seneca Country and to destroy every form of property and food, utterly devastating the Indian country.

The Hollocaust. After an attack at Newtown (near the present Elmira), the news spread that the American troops were coming, and, as the army approached, one by one the Seneca towns were abandoned. Sullivan caused the destruction of every town and hamlet that he found, burned the food supplies and cut down orchards and growing crops. The stricken Seneca were torn by fearful emotions, and, when they caught Lieutenant Boyd and Parker, they tortured Boyd after mutilating him. Parker was decapitated. The torture of Boyd is one of the most revolting in the annals of Seneca warfare, and his death may be laid to the door of the British Officer, Colonel Butler, who might have saved him had he obeyed even the elemental instincts of humanity and granted his appeal to human consideration, but Butler was an infamous character.

21. Results of Sullivan's Expedition.

The Seneca Flee. In the end the Seneca fled where they might, most of them westward over the Niagara trail and to the protecting gates on Fort Niagara. This was an unexpected drain upon the resources of the British stronghold, and one upon which they had not counted. It was now difficult to obtain supplies from Canada and the Indians were fed on scanty rations* until spring, when they were induced to move to secure places along the Cattaraugus, Tonawanda and Alleghany. Numbers returned to the Genesee country to prowl for awhile among the ashes of their old homes, and then to build anew in other spots.

Had Sullivan's successful army pushed on to Niagara, there is little doubt that he would have captured the fort and have justly punished those who better deserved chastisement than the misguided Indians.

A Decisive Victory. Sullivan's punitive expedition has been described many times, and varying estimates of its value given. That it was a decisive campaign there can be no doubt. It proved the power of American arms over the Iroquois Confederacy, it warned the British that the "provincials" were able to cope with

*It is said that certain British officers poisoned the Indian refugees to reduce the drain upon rations.

military problems, and it put an end to border depredations by the Seneca. It was more than this, it was an outstanding achievement of the Revolutionary war.

Sullivan's expedition opened the Genesee Country to the white man and revealed it a paradise of fertility and productiveness. It opened up a domain of highly desirable soil, and Sullivan's men never forgot it, but, when the war was over, clamored to return that they might build homes and rear mills and towns in this Eden of the New World.

Broadhead's Campaign. Sullivan was not alone in an expedition against the Indians, for Colonel Broadhead left Pittsburgh on August 11, 1799, on a similar campaign against the Alleghany Seneca, traveling four hundred miles, destroying one hundred and thirty-five Indian houses and laying waste to vast fields and orchards. He scattered the Seneca, the Muncey and Mingo, and returned without the loss of a single man. Thus in the Genesee Country from end to end were battles and expeditions of the Revolutionary war fought out to successful conclusions. The red men had seen the new flag and learned to repect it, for where it came British power vanished.

When one considers the subject, he must see that the forces of the American States laid hold of western New York and expelled the Seneca and their allies almost without a contest. Had this been the triumph of most nations, the title to the soil would have been considered extinguished and the land claimed by conquest. The Seneca, however, though scattered and humbled, did not admit defeat, and the trees with twisted tops which they left along the line of their retreat, symbolized that "the power of the whirlwind may be great but the tree still stands, though its branches are twisted and broken". It was their promise to return and reclaim their land.

Plate 19. Solomon Obail. A descendant of Cornplanter. This photograph was taken at the Pan-American exposition in 1900. The chief showed little trace of his European blood, which was probably about one-eighth.

The Readjustment. The year 1780 was one of a home-return for the Seneca, and they went back to Big Tree, Canawagus and the scattered places along the upper waters of the Genesee, as at Canadea and Squawkie Hill. Others pushed further westward, many of the Beardstown people settling along the Tonawanda, others going down the Alleghany, and still others pushing westward into Ohio into the mixed settlements on the Sandusky. The bitterness of defeat still rankled, and those who had revenge to nurse sought bloody comfort in the service of Brant and the Tory raiders south of the Mohawk.

By 1781, the Seneca, Cayuga and Onondaga refugees, from their rendezvous at Niagara began to settle on Buffalo creek, the first to establish himself being none other than Old King Sayenqueraghta. Buffalo was thus largely settled by the eastern Seneca, that is, those of the purest Seneca descent.

V. SENECA POWER WANES.

England Forgets. In the Treaty of Peace, which closed the Revolutionary contest, Great Britain forgot her Iroquois allies, and no stipulations whatsoever were made for their protection. This placed them in a most hazardous situation, for the citizens of the new United States still remembered the horrors of border warfare. That the Indians should go was the general will. Washington and Philip Schuyler were inclined to be more lenient and sought to devise means for conciliating the Six Nations.

1. The Treaty of Fort Stanwix.

The First Treaty. Though Washington had directed the punitive campaign of Sullivan, winning for himself the name, Town Destroyer, once the end had been achieved, he was still moved with pity for these deluded people, so grievously betrayed by scheming British agents. A plan was devised by which the Seneca with their allies, except the Mohawk, might retain a portion of their ancient homeland. To define what they still should hold, and to consummate the terms of peace, the Treaty of Fort Stanwix was devised and signed (1784). It was the first treaty with any Indian tribe made by the United States of America. Though it took from them large portions of their western lands and fixed a western boundary, the Seneca, and their allies, reluctantly signed the document. Success in this effort came largely through the importunities of Cornplanter, who saw that peace on ample acres was far more to be desired than war upon a wider range of territory that could not be defended. Red Jacket argued the might and supremacy of the Six Nations, and railed against the provisions of the treaty, but in the end, though the Indians were deeply stirred by his eloquence, Cornplanter's wisdom prevailed. The treaty was signed by a few chiefs, but not by a majority. It was accepted, however, by the Six Nations, though the Seneca could not be reconciled to the losses they had sustained. To this day they have scarcely recovered from their feeling that injustice was done.

Attitude of the Commissioners. The United States believed that the provisions were liberal considering the relations of and differences between the contracting parties, and the Commissioners were careful to convey the idea to the Indians that the land was given back to them through mercy and fatherly consideration alone, and not because it was necessary or a matter of compulsion. The Commissioners took a haughty position, for were they not representatives of a conquering nation? By this attitude they hoped to impress the Indians with their advantageous position and to make them feel the weakness of the Indian cause. The Iroquois stalwartly insisted that they were yet an independent people, but the Commissioners denied this, and asserted the supreme sovereignty of the State and Nation. The failure of the Indians to agree upon this, even now, causes complications.

Attitude of the Seneca. As the years went on the Treaty of Fort Stanwix became a source of great irritation to the Seneca and their allied tribesmen. Defeat, starvation and homelessness were bad enough, but this treaty was humiliation indeed. Said Cornplanter later: "You told us that we were in your hand, and that by closing it you could crush us to nothing, and you demanded from us a great country as the price of that peace you had offered us,—as if our want of strength had destroyed our rights. Our chiefs had felt your power and were unable to contend against you, and they therefore gave up that country. What they agreed to has bound our nation, but your anger against us must by this time be cooled, and though our strength has not increased nor your power become less, we ask you to consider calmly, *were the terms dictated to us by your Commissioners reasonable and just?**

Washington's Humanity. Fort Stanwix became the place of almost daily councils relating to the dissatisfaction of the Seneca. Red Jacket kept up a constant agitation and, by his fiery oratory, awakened his people to an understanding of what they had lost. The Treaty of Fort Harmer on the Muskingum followed in 1789, and all through these trying events we hear the voice of George Washington endeavoring to mollify the Six Nations and to assure them that the United States meant to accord full justice. Washington's magnanimity is little less than astonishing, and his gentle firmness and diplomacy make his policy one of the triumphs of statesmanship. This the Six Nations afterward realized, and their religious leaders have accorded him an honorable place in their "Happy Hunting Ground,"—yet a solitary place, for they said that he was the only white man who could enter the Indians' heaven. They remember Washington with equal gratitude today and he is mentioned with reverence in their native feasts.

Border Wars. To add to the difficulties of the first decade, a border war started in Pennsylvania and Virginia, culminating in the murder of several Seneca chiefs and head men by Pennsylvania bordermen. This was the occasion for renewal of hostile feeling against the United States, a state of mind that was encouraged by British tories. The Six Nations, though humbled, it was realized, were capable of terrible reprisals should they take the war trail again. The Federal Government

*Public Documents, Indians' Affairs, Vol. 1, pp. 206-207. Quoted by Stone, Life of Red Jacket, p. 29.

at once took measures to disavow responsibility for the murder of the Indians and offered a reward for the arrest of the culprits.

Royal Grants. The Indians now saw the results of an astonishing code of European law. Little did they know that unknown to them under a royal grant their domain had been given to the Massachusetts Bay Colony (Plymouth Company), by a King who never owned it and never saw it, to a colony that never saw it and could not use it. Nor did they know that it had been again granted to the Duke of York by Charles I. These conflicting grants caused serious difficulty after the war, for the states that grew out of the colonies inherited their rights. New York and Massachusetts were thus in conflict. To adjudicate the case a convention was held at Hartford in December, 1786. As a result the State of Massachusetts ceded to the State of New York all her claim to the government, sovereignty and jurisdiction of the territory lying west of her present west boundary line. New York, as her part of the bargain, ceded to Massachusetts the preemption right, or fee, of the land, *subject to the title of the natives.* This cession was subject to certain exceptions, for New York claimed title to portions of land within this six million acre tract. One notable reservation was a mile-wide strip of land east of and adjoining the eastern bank of the Niagara river, and extending its whole length. The State claimed the land to the river's edge, for the Seneca had agreed to this, but, inasmuch as they did not sell the bed of the river, they still claim ownership to the Niagara, from its east bank to the international line. What will the power companies reply to this? Probably much, but not to the Seneca, save, "Get it if you can".

Land Purchases. New York thus acquired the right to govern this part of its territory and Massachusetts secured the right to sell the land. This right it sold in 1788 to Nathaniel Gorham and Oliver Phelps, both citizens of Massachusetts, for one million dollars, payable in three annual installments. The Phelps and Gorham Company received their contract of sale in April, and in June held a treaty with the Indians on Buffalo creek, by which they bought the Indian claim to about 2,600,000 acres on the eastern side of "the purchase". This agreement successfully achieved, Massachusetts conveyed and quit claimed all right and title to Oliver Phelps and Nathaniel Gorham.

2. The Pickering Treaty.

The account of these land transactions is thoroughly interesting, but it forms no major part of our paper.   Our concern is rather with the extinguishment of the Indian title, and with the treaties that effected this.   We have seen that the Seneca were not satisfied with the Fort Stanwix agreement and that they were stirred by affairs on the western border.   It was evident that a new treaty should be arranged, if peace was to be established.

Early Treaties. Washington therefore selected Colonel Timothy Pickering as his Commissioner and charged him with the duty of making a new treaty that should satisfy both settler and Indian.   A great council was convoked at Tioga Point in which many tribes gathered to pour out their grievances and lay bare their hearts. It is here that we catch glimpses of the character and eloquence of Red Jacket, Farmer's Brother, Little Billy, Fish Carrier and Henry Apamaut, the Mohikan. Later came the Proctor Council at Buffalo creek and then the Pickering Council at Painted Post.   During all these events British agents had kept the Indians in a state of agitation, and western tribes sought to unite the Six Nations in a league that might destroy the colonies and push the American settler back into the sea, from whence he came.

For many reasons the United States wished to cultivate the friendship of the Six Nations, but not the least desire was to be humane and just. A friendly council was called at Philadelphia and all noted chiefs bidden to attend. To it they came in all their ceremony and dignity, and were met by a colorful display of military pomp. They were paraded and feasted and hailed as friends, loaded with presents and clothing, and feasted again. One chief even died from an over-abundance of good food, and, at this day we may suspect, of good rum.

Timothy Pickering. Colonel Pickering headed this task of instilling faith and hope in the hearts of the Indians, and by his acts he sought to develop a feeling of real loyalty to the new council of states,—the Thirteen Fires. To him was committed a great task. As a constructive factor in American history Pickering should be better known. Born in Salem, Massachusetts, in 1766 he was commissioned a Lieutenant. Ten years later he was a regimental commander in the American Army. His deportment won the esteem of General Knox and commended itself even to Washington. His attainments as a lawyer and military commander gave him large influence, but beyond these qualifications he had a pleasing personality and a stalwart, athletic physique, being six feet high, broad of shoulder, of dignified and almost regal bearing. As a commissioner to the Indians he was an ideal choice, for the Indians like to measure a man by the respect he instinctively commands, and by the natural confidence that he instills. The Indians felt Pickering's sincerity and named him Connisauti, meaning "The Sunny Side of the Hill". The name was an ancient and honorable one among them

and aptly applied, though genuine Indian names seldom
have any personal application. Pickering with rare
sympathy felt that the Seneca and their brethren were
in a most unhappy state of mind. Divesting himself of
prejudice he was able to interpret their acts and their
situation, in accordance with the times in which they
lived and the cultural state in which they were reared,
and herein lay his success.

3. The Canandaigua Treaty.

To settle all differences that existed between the
Six Nations and their white neighbors, to finally cement
peace, to declare the intention of the United States and
to fix boundaries definitely, a new council was held at
Canandaigua during the late autumn of 1794. It was
the culmination of a long series of events, some of which
we have mentioned all too briefly. Long and stormy
were these final deliberations. Each great chief had his
day in court and even the women spoke. There were
feastings and exchanges of mutual good will, but at
times it seemed as if the council would fail. The Seneca,
though they expressed a desire to be friendly, had a
certain haughtiness, for they knew that some of their
western friends had united against General Anthony
Wayne, who was following up the victories of the
Indians over Harmer and St. Clair, but during the
Canandaigua proceedings, a Tuscarora runner brought
in the news of Wayne's victory over Little Turtle and his
Miami warriors. Sukachgooh, the Black Snake, as
Wayne was called by the red man, had coiled about his
foes and crushed them. The news had a salutary effect
upon the council.

The Pickering Treaty. The council continued its
deliberations, Red Jacket generally objecting to any
move to relinquish hold on a single mile of land on this
side of the Ohio. Red Jacket, however, was a war chief

Plate 20. Caroline **Mountpleasant** (Ji-gon-sa-seh). Mrs. Mountpleasant was a Tonawanda Seneca and a sister of General Parker. She
inherited the title of "the Mother of Nations" or "Peace Queen," and
fittingly lived on the site of the old Neutral town of refuge on the
Tuscarora reservation. She was the wife of Chief Mountpleasant. Born
1824, died 1891.

of inferior rank, and not a sachem. He made up by his oratory what he lacked in station, and thus was regarded as a power among his people. Fortunately for the white people of the Genesee, Clear Sky was the presiding sachem of the Seneca at this council, and the voices of Cornplanter and Farmer's Brother conveyed messages that were more logical and conciliatory. The Seneca gave up their Ohio lands and agreed to new boundaries; the other nations had their lines defined accurately, and all were assured the right to hold and possess their remaining belongings until such a time as they might choose to sell to the people of the United States.

The treaty as signed reads in part:

Article 1. Peace and friendship are hereby firmly established and shall be perpetual between the United States of America and the Six Nations.

Article 2. The United States acknowledge the land reserved to the Oneida, Cayuga and Onondaga nations, in their respective treaties with the State of New York and called their reservations, to be their property; and the United States will never claim the same nor disturb them or either of the Six Nations, nor their Indian friends residing thereon, and united with them, in the free use and enjoyment thereof; but said reservations shall remain theirs until they choose to sell the same to the people of the United States who have the right to purchase.

Article 3. The land of the Seneca Nation is bounded as follows (here follows the description)— and the United States will never claim the same, nor disturb the Seneca nation, but it shall remain theirs until they choose to sell to the people of the United States who have the right to purchase.

Other articles provided for the construction of a wagon road from Fort Schlosser to Buffalo creek, the free and unobstructed passage of the people of the United States through their lands, the free use of water-

ways and harbors adjoining their lands, and, what was
of vast importance, the giving up of private retaliation
for judicial arrest and trial. This placed the punishment of Iroquois criminals at the discretion of Federal
Courts.

Peace was now assured, and the points of disagree-
ment settled. The Seneca felt that, though they had
lost a vast territory west of the Pennsylvania line,
they had in lieu acquired lasting peace and a promise
that what they now had was theirs forever. Said one
of the chiefs to Colonel Pickering, "This settlement
appears as a great light to me!" And, indeed this treaty
remains a light, being the basic document upon which
the Six Nations rest their land titles and tribal rights.

Results of the New Treaty. Soon after the Canandaigua treaty, Anthony Wayne concluded the treaty of
Grenville and by this the western Indians were pacified.
The Six Nations now felt that they might rest in full
security. They were assured that their white neighbors
would be kind and peaceable, and to similar conduct they
had also pledged themselves. No longer would their
young warriors have a plausible excuse to take the war
trail westward to join hostile bands that harried the
settlers, and now the old people might live and die without the continual fear of bloodshed, sudden attack and
starvation. The readjustment to the new era had come.
To the settlers in the newly opened country this meant
that safety was an assured state. The land companies
immediately became busy and the population increased
by leaps and bounds. Towns sprang up and with them
newspapers, inns, stores and schools and with these
things the dawn of a cultural life.

4. Location of Reservations.

Seneca Reservations. Our concern, however, is
with the aboriginal occupation. Let us glance for a

moment at the tracts of land that were assured to them as the new century dawned.   The Phelps and Gorham Purchase had stripped the Seneca of all their eastern lands, save a small section of Genesee valley land lying against the river and south of a line dropped to the Pennsylvania line from Little Beard's Town to the point where the Genesee river enters the State of New York. This purchase also took in lands west of the river from a point about fifteen miles west of Canawagus and running fifteen degrees east of north to Lake Ontario. This was but a small portion of their ancient domain and conquests, but even this was more than they could occupy and improve.   This attracted the Robert Morris Purchase by which all this land, with twelve exceptions, was passed over to the Morris company.   These exceptions are of much interest to us because they will reveal where the Seneca were.   A glance at the map will be helpful here as a guide to locations.

1.   The Canawagus reservation was on the west side of the Genesee opposite the present town of Avon. This tract faced the river for one mile and ran back two miles from it.

2.   The Big Tree Reservation was at the village of Big Tree and also contained two square miles, running west from the river.

3.   Little Beard's Reservation, also of two square miles, lay just south of Big Tree.   Both Big Tree and Little Beard's were opposite the present site of Geneseo, and the Seneca, in speaking of these two locations, always refer to them as Geneseo (in their sonorous language, Djoh-nes-io).   Here dwelt many descendants of Huron captives.

4.   Squawkie Hill Reservation touched the river at one corner and embraced two square miles.   Within

it were Squawkie Hill and Big Kettle towns. Here lived many Shawnee and Sauk captives and their descendants.

5. Gardeau Flats Reservation, where at one time was the home of Mary Jemison, was the largest of the Genesee tracts, and lay on both sides of the river in nearly equal areas. It contained 17,927 acres.

6. Caneadea, officially called Kaounadeau, was at the bend of the Genesee in the present Allegany county. It was two miles wide and eight miles long, being a perfect parallelogram. Its southern line crossed the river at right angles and it lay to the northeast. Its area was 10,240 acres.

7. Oil Spring Reservation of 640 acres was carelessly omitted from the Big Tree Treaty, though it was the intention of Robert Morris to include it. It was subsequently given to the Seneca by court order (1856). It lies in Allegany county within the forks of Oil creek. The celebrated oil spring here was one source of the renowned "Seneca Oil".

8. Buffalo Creek Reservation was a large tract nearly one hundred and thirty square miles. Its favored location along Lake Erie and upon Buffalo creek, and upon several other streams, made it a highly desirable tract, and one which because of its evident commercial advantages later led white men to wrest it from its Indian possessors.

9. Tonawanda Reservation, embracing more than seventy square miles, lay along Tonawanda creek. It was an oblong with its north-west and its south-east corners indented, a symbol that the white man's wedge was to split it into a still smaller area.

10. The Alleghany River Reservation lay along the Alleghany river for forty miles, a half mile on each

side of the stream. It was the wildest and most inaccessible of all the Indian lands.

11. The Cattaraugus Reservation lay along Cattaraugus creek from its mouth to a line running north and south some seventeen miles up-stream. It was a well chosen location and upon it was one of the ancient towns, named after the creek, Cattaraugus.

12. The Canadaway Reservation was another small tract at the mouth of the Canadaway creek along Lake Erie, just west of Cattaraugus, and lay in Chautauqua county.

Reservation Life. In these twelve tracts, some large and some small, the Seneca people sought to fit themselves. Though much of their territory had been dissipated, they no longer needed large hunting ranges, owing to the great changes in their economic situation. Agriculture began to play its part once more, and Seneca farms became larger. Communal village life and harvesting almost totally vanished.

No longer was it necessary to find secluded spots for their villages, and to interpose vast stretches between themselves and their enemies. Thus the shrinking of their lands and a localizing of their holdings, even though only a small fraction of their original domain, had its advantages. An assured peace began to bring a new prosperity, and one far unlike the old, even in its most glorious days. And still,—the new era was not of their making, so far as its economics was concerned. In this respect the Seneca were forced to wear a borrowed culture, just as they now took by choice the white man's clothing and implements. Even so, the gun was more effective than the bow, and the brass cauldron more durable than the clay kettle.

It will be seen that the original village life of the

Seneca was greatly disturbed by the new order. A gregarious people were now spread out thin in a far-flung country. Their hamlets were small, and the health conditions deplorable. Their only escape was to find the forest again, and there rear their lonely cabins. Thus there was a constant ebb and flow of population, and for awhile it was an ebb with a heavy under-tow, for smallpox and yellow fever played havoc with them.

And so the Seneca nation, composed of the remnants of a score of broken tribes, sought to adjust itself to the white man's way. They were at first confused and their progress was not remarkable. Their lands lay largely uncultivated,—and therefore a constant temptation to the more thrifty settler who yearned to nose his plowshare in the rich, mellow loam.

Soon the Seneca were again to face an insistent demand for their lands; they were to discover that the term "forever" merely meant as long as one or both parties to the contract saw fit to keep their original intention. The Holland Land Company began its importunities, and then the Ogden Land Company.

5. Conspiracies of Land Companies.

Land Frauds. In 1838 the Ogden Land Company, aided and abetted by a United States Commissioner, sought to secure the remaining lands of the Seneca and induce them to emigrate to other lands in Kansas, secured from certain western tribes.

Seneca chiefs were importuned night and day, bribed, drugged and plied with liquor, but the consent of a majority to this infamous pact could not be secured. At length the Company was reduced to the necessity of taking debauched Indians to Buffalo and penning them in an inn where they were "elected and declared chiefs" by company agents, and then for pay forced to sign the treaty. Not a single wary Tonawanda Chief could be kidnapped, bribed or induced to touch the rum of the unscrupulous agents, yet their names were forged to the document, and they appeared upon it as having agreed to sell out and leave for the uncertain west. The Seneca had discovered the subtleness of a new form of warfare.

Quaker Defenders. The Quakers and many other conscientious people of western New York protested in vain. Notwithstanding all the revelations of missionaries as to the criminal methods used to gain their ends, the Ogden Land Company rushed the forged treaty to Washington, where it was hastily ratified by the Senate. The Indian delegate, Two Guns, went by stage coach to the Capitol with a protest signed by nearly all the voters and women of his nation, but he was followed and his satchel stolen by spies who followed in his track.

The Quakers headed by Philip Thomas did everything within their power to expose the transactions and their committee, "— *became thoroughly satisfied with the revolting fact that in order to drive these poor Indians from their lands deception and fraud had been practiced to an extent, perhaps, without parallel in the dark history of oppression and wrong to which the aborigines of our country have been subjected.*"

The extensive reports of the Society of Friends, printed from 1838 to 1856, afford interesting reading along these lines. The Friends did not give up the fight until an amended treaty of 1842 had been made, by which the Seneca might receive back Alleghany and Cattaraugus, but must lose all other lands including Buffalo and Tonawanda. The Tonawanda who were not parties to this treaty found themselves expatriated, and their lands sold over their heads without having had a

word to say except that of protest.   Years after, it was
in 1856, after the Ogden Company had tried in vain to
dispossess them, they bought back their land at $20.00
an acre, after having been forced to part with it at twenty
cents an acre, but their purchase was of only one-tenth
their former holdings.   The Seneca people found that it
paid to be honorable and peaceful,—but not much,—if
its reward was computed.

It must not be thought that the law-abiding citizens
of western New York looked kindly on these frauds, for
their names are found upon numerous petitions of
protest.   The Seneca had untiring friends in Philip
Thomas, the Quaker, and in Dr. Asher Wright, the
American Board Missionary at Buffalo Creek.   These
bravely led the fight and mustered the protests of the
citizen communities, but in vain.   Many Indians were
embittered so deeply that they said, *"If this be an act of
a Christian Nation, we will cling to the faith of our fathers
and reject Christianity forever."*   The strength of the
non-Christian party of the Six Nations dates from the
fraudulent treaty, and to this day they recite the frauds
of Buffalo creek as a reason why Christians should not
be trusted.

The Seneca in the War of 1812.   This method of
acquiring Indian lands was poor reward, indeed, for the
services of the Seneca in the War of 1812.   When the
settlers were anxiously awaiting the action of the Seneca
Nation and fearing a renewal of border hostilities, for
British agents were still active, and the Seneca had
provocation enough, the Indian relieved the suspense by
declaring war on Great Britain, and mustered their forces
to meet invasion.   As allies of the United States they
placed their forces, led by their own captains, under General Porter.   Well they fought at Black Rock, Lundy's

Plate 21. General Ely Samuel Parker (Do-ne-ho-ga-wa). General Parker was a Tonawanda Seneca of the Wolf Clan, and for many years the leading civil chief of his people. He was a civil engineer and architect, later joining General Grant and becoming his military secretary. Born 1826, died 1892.

Plate 22. Edward Cornplanter (So-son-do-wa). Councilor and High Priest of the Cattaraugus Seneca. He was an able and intelligent leader of the non-Christian party of the Six Nations. Born c. 1852, died 1918.

Lane, Chippewa and at Buffalo, so effectively that
General Scott commended them for their manly way of
fighting. No longer did they scalp the dead or torture
prisoners, for though Colonel Farmer's Brother was in
command, his tactics of warfare had undergone a great
change since the day he led his band of young warriors
at Devil's Hole.*

For their loyal services the Seneca had a right to
expect better treatment from the country than that
which was accorded them at Buffalo creek in 1838, for
they had proven their good faith and had even fought
their own kinsmen, who had gone to Canada under
Joseph Brant and established a Canadian Six Nations
Confederacy on the banks of the Grand river in Ontario.
It was long before the breach between the two divisions
was healed, and as late as 1876 at the dedication of the
Caneadea council house in Letchworth Park, it was
difficult to induce the Mohawk, Colonel W. S. Kerr, to
shake hands with Solomon Obail, the descendant of
Cornplanter.   Yet, through the kindly persuasion of
William Prior Letchworth, the two did grasp hands and
pledge their friendship.

After the calamity at Buffalo the Indians began to
abandon their homes, their little villages, their mission
church and the graves of their fathers,—the graves of
Red Jacket, Farmer's Brother, Little Billy and scores
of others who went to their eternal sleep in the Buffalo
valley.   Again an exodus was on.

6. The Attenuation of Seneca Blood.

A Mixed Race. The Seneca of this period were a
mixed people, and no less than twenty broken tribes
were incorporate with them, chiefly the Delaware,

---

*For a full account of the Seneca in the War of 1812, see "Life of
General Ely S. Parker," Vol. XXIII, Buffalo Historical Society, 1919.

Mohican or Munsee, Fox, Cherokee, Nanticoke, Shawnee, Wyandot, Neutral, Erie, Mingo and Chippewa. At first, though all were known as Seneca for official classification, tribal derivation was remembered. Philip Kenjockety, a venerable and influential chief, was a descendant of the Neutral Nation, Blue Eye was a Cherokee, John Armstrong was a Delaware, Silverheels was a Shawnee, Tall Chief was a Fox.

Mixed bloods were numerous. Captain Pollard was the son of an English trader of that name, though the Captain was usually known by his Seneca name, Ga-on-da-wa-neh, *Big Tree*. He was a man of sterling character, "—one of the most honest, pure minded, worthy men I ever knew," wrote Orlando Allen, and Horatio Jones, who knew him intimately, said of him, "Morally speaking, Pollard was as good a man as any white minister that ever lived."

Major Jack Berry was also the son of an English trader who lived near Avon, but the Major made his home at Squawkie Hill. He was a man of unusual intellect and spoke English fluently, frequently acting as interpreter for Red Jacket, whom he ardently admired. It was Major Berry who dropped the hint of advice that helped Horatio Jones run his gauntlet successfully.

John Montour was a son of Queen Catherine, a half blood French woman whose settlement at the head of Seneca lake was a well known location, being one of the first towns destroyed by Sullivan after leaving Newtown. John Montour was one of the refugees at Fort Niagara after the raid, and from having eaten some of the poisoned flour given as rations to his people, developed an ulcerated lip which in time ate it entirely away. This mutilation gave him a fierce appearance, though in reality he was a mild mannered and pleasant man.

7. White Captives.

White Captives. In their border raids the Seneca warriors took many white captives, expecting to adopt them as their own children. This was a horrible experience to many, and there are many heartrending accounts of unhappy captives, who during long years of endeavor, sought to find their relatives. The narrative of the Gilbert captivity is a specific case, that of Frances Slocum, the lost sister, another, but each story has a different ending.

It is impossible to tell how many French, English, Dutch and American men and women, boys and girls were captured and hidden by the Seneca. We know that there were many, but no complete account has ever been made. Now and then we catch a glimpse of captives, as travelers passed through Seneca settlements, as in the case of Kanadesaga (Old Castle, near Geneva), where Cornplanter lived with a white wife, and where Sullivan found a white baby that could not speak a word of English. In every Seneca town there were half-blood children of French and English traders. The Swiss gunsmith at Old Castle had a Seneca wife. Thus, through captives and by the inter-marriage of forest dwellers and wanderers, Seneca blood by the middle of the eighteenth century was becoming diluted with that of the European.

Mary Jemison. By far the most reliable and interesting story of a captivity is that of Mary Jemison, the White Woman of the Genesee, whose biography, taken down by Dr. James Everett Seaver in November, 1823, has passed through more than twenty editions. It is not our intention to review the life of this remarkable woman, but to call attention to the fact, that once she resigned herself to her fate, Mary Jemison did not find her lot a hard one or unendurable. Her Indian friends loved her and she probably suffered no more hardships than she would as a frontier woman among her own people. Her life was a *useful* one and her example of thrift and industry had a marked influence upon her adopted people, who in the end rewarded her well. By the fortunate circumstance of Dr. Seaver's record of her life, taken substantially from her own lips, we have a record of Seneca life during the period, 1775-1823, that is without equal in its value as an interpretation of the times.

Parrish and Jones. Jasper Parrish was another captive whose influence was of large importance in the molding of events in the Genesee country. At the age of eleven years he was captured by a party of Delaware, who perhaps had lost kinsmen in the Wyoming massacre. Young Parrish was passed from one tribe to another, and during his varied experience learned five or six Indian dialects. His prudence and good judgment, united with his sense of humor, gained many friends for him, and he was everywhere a favorite. One of his fellow captives was Horatio Jones, who in 1781 was taken prisoner.

Horatio Jones, unlike Parrish, though young, was a soldier, and might have shared a soldier's fate at the hands of his enemies. By good fortune, however, he was ordered to run the gauntlet, the goal being a wigwam which, if it should be reached, would mean safety. Warriors and youths lined up on either side of the path and, as Jones ran by, pelted him with stones, clubs, javelins and arrows, but the white boy was a swiftly moving mark, and he skillfully dodged the missiles, escaping uninjured. His pleasant manner and sense of humor gained him great admiration. His tormentors among the young warriors of the village soon found him more than a match for them. When Sharp Shins, for example, threw tomahawks at him, he tossed them back with such fatal accuracy that he nearly killed him. He once thrust a boiling squash under the shirt of another warrior, who teased him beyond the limits of endurance, and the Seneca who witnessed the prank laughed long and loud. They admired a man who gave more than he received, and did so with a smile.

Both Parrish and Jones endeared themselves to the Seneca and, when by the Treaty of Fort Stanwix all prisoners were released, the Indians gave up these two with many a misgiving. These young men had found their mission in life and soon returned to their Seneca friends, both commissioned by the United States Government as Interpreters. Jones settled at Little Beard's Town and Parrish made his home at Canandaigua. They married white wives and reared large families,— though Jones had an Indian family also.

Rewards for Faithful Service. At the Genesee council of 1798, it was ordered that both Jones and Parrish should receive substantial presents. Farmer's Brother made an eloquent address which was designed to be communicated to the Legislature of New York, asking a confirmation of the title of the land given them. In his address Farmer's Brother said, among other things:

"Brothers: This whirlwind (the Revolutionary War) was so directed by the Great Spirit above, as to throw into our arms two of your infant children, Horatio Jones and Jasper Parrish. We adopted them into our families, and made them our children. We nourished them and loved them. They lived with us many years. At length the Great Spirit spoke to the whirlwind, and it was still. A clear and uninterrupted sky appeared, the path of peace was opened, and the chain of friendship was once more made bright. Then these adopted children left us to seek their relations. We wished them to return among us and promised, if they would return and live in our country, to give each of them a seat of land for them and their children to sit down upon.

"*Brothers*: They have returned and have for several years past been serviceable to us as interpreters; we still feel our hearts beat with affection for them and now wish to fulfill the promise we made them for their services."

Farmer's Brother then outlined the tracts of land assigned to Jones and Parrish on Suyguquoydes creek near the Niagara. It was a generous gift and characteristic as an expression of gratitude. Of Jones and Parrish and Farmer's Brother we shall learn more in pages that tell of the treaties that followed the war.

Life of Captives. In many cases, therefore, the life of captives, or those who had been in captivity, was not an unhappy one. Misery mostly came when the captive had been torn from those to whom he was closely attached, and could not adapt himself to Indian ways. Once the captive began to look for the sunny side of aboriginal life, he generally found it enjoyable. This was so true that it was frequently almost impossible to persuade captives to return to civilization.

An instance is recorded by the French traveler, Chateaubriand, who hearing that one of his countrymen lived with the Indians, visited him with the intent of discussing his situation. After a lengthy conversation Chateaubriand asked the question toward which his inquiries had been directed.

"Philip, are you happy?" he asked.

"Happy!" ejaculated the prisoner, smiling at his wide freedom of life and lack of artificial shackles, "Happy? Yes, happy, but happy only since I became a savage."

The truth is that this wilderness life among

the natives had its pleasant side. We have been accusomed to think of it as one of tragedies only, for our history of our Indian contacts has been mostly that of war. If we should construct our own national story from the incidents that took place in the wake of armies, red with gore, our own history would become a sad picture. Thus, the internal life of an Indian tribe in times of peace was not devoid of a condition in which real happiness might be found. The Indians at home were kind and considerate, hospitable and genial. We will recall the sentiment of Roger Williams in his "Key":

"If Nature's sonnes both wild and tame
      humane and courteous be,
How ill becomes the sonnes of God to want
      humanity!"

8. The Seneca Indians Since 1838.

Seneca Reservations. The Seneca people now occupy three principal reservations in New York State. Those who followed Brant into Canada live on the Six Nations tract and form a minor group. Those who wandered into Ohio united with the mixed tribes along the Sandusky, and some went on to Oklahoma, where they have a small settlement today. It is possible that these are mostly of Huron-Erie blood, and are merely the descendants of captives. Their location is in the Wyandot agency, in the north-east corner of the state.

Land and Population. In New York, where more than three thousand still dwell, there are two divisions of them,—the Seneca Nation and the Tonawanda band. Each has a different status. The Tonawanda people, numbering some five hundred, own their land in fee, having purchased it with the blood-money they received from their stolen acres, disposed of by the Ogden Land Company of infamous record. The Seneca Nation occupies the Cattaraugus reservation and the Allegany reservation. The former lies along Cattaraugus creek and is in parts of Cattaraugus, Erie and Chautauqua counties. This reservation embraces 21,680 acres, a portion of it being fertile bottom land. The Cattaraugus people number about 2,200 souls. The Allegany reservation lies wholly in southern Cattaraugus county, stretching along the Alleghany river for forty miles.

The city of Salamanca lies in the heart of this reservation and is built on land leased for ninety-nine years. There are five other villages on this reservation. The reservation area is 30,469 acres and there is a population of about nine hundred and fifty souls.

These people live for the most part like their rural white neighbors, cultivating the soil and raising stock. Some are excellent farmers, but many have no taste for agriculture,—in this respect being like their neighbors of European stock. Some are mechanics, some small merchants, some showmen; others are clerks and machinists.

On the reservations only a few have amassed any considerable fortune. Some are reputed to own paying stock in corporations, and some make a comfortable living by selling milk and farm produce. Still others rent their lands to the more thrifty, or lease their acres to the surrounding farmers, citizen and alien.

Musicians. Indian homes today are usually small, but the women are neat housekeepers and excellent cooks, as a rule. Most of the men are good musicians, and there have been times when as many as four or five brass bands flourished on the Cattaraugus reservation, alone. In those days there were several well known band leaders, among them A. Sim Logan, Chester

Plate 23. Black Squirrel, a Tonawanda Seneca veteran of the War of 1812.

C. Lay, Orlando Doxtater, Alfred Logan. In later years leaders in musical circles were Sylvester Douglas Lay, T. Francis Jemison, Charles Wilson, and others. There were also some noted singers among them, Henry Pierce (bass), Kosuth Bishop (baritone), and Avery Gordon (bass). Musicians and singers are still to be found among them.

The Seneca are still inclined toward athletics, and their constant practice at lacrosse and baseball (which may have had an Indian origin), give play to the muscles of their youth. Among the famous runners of the early sixties was Deerfoot (Louis Bennet), who ran races in the London Crystal Palace. In later years there were the Pierce boys, of whom Frank was perhaps the most noted. One of these brothers, Bemis, was a noted Carlisle football player, and at one time was coach of Kenyon college.

Indian homes of all classes are like thousands of homes found throughout rural communities. In them are found books, magazines and the daily papers. Education has done much to bring about a better understanding of the "white man's way". Mission schools and churches have played their part in the "civilizing" process. The old life has all but departed, save for the little communities where the followers of Handsome Lake dwell, but even these only enact their old rites when festal occasions appear upon their aboriginal calendar.

These Indians now have comforts and luxuries in their homes, as washing machines, gas stoves, phonographs, radios, telephones and milk separators. The daily rural delivery passes their doors, telegrams reach them, they eat their meals to the sound of music wirelessed by radio from the Waldorf-Astoria or the Bellevue-Stratford,—and they like it.

The Seneca still love horses, but many of them have automobiles. During my visit to one of the council houses as a State Indian Commissioner in 1920, each of the sixteen Seneca councilors came in an automobile that cost $900 or more, for there were Franklins, Packards, Paiges and Willys-Knights.

Three-quarters of these people are professed Christians, the Presbyterian church claiming the larger share, and next the Baptist and the Methodist and the Disciples, —the latter coming in about 1923, building their little church in a single day. The fourth quarter are non-Christian followers of the Prophet, and oddly enough these conservative people live closest to their white neighbors. The three Seneca Long Houses all stand within ear-shot of locomotive whistles.

Numerous Seneca men and women live in citizen communities, where they make their living as the white man does. Some are doing well, but those who fail still have the old reservation to which they may return, to rest and recuperate. It is a refuge for those who find civilization in its intensity a bit too disconcerting. There are Seneca Indians now in almost every state of the Union, and in many of the important cities. It has been estimated that there are about sixty living in Rochester, at least that number in Buffalo, and even a score in New York.

9. Seneca Claims on Western New York.

A $2,800,000,000 Claim. During the past three or four years (say beginning with 1922), a movement has been started by certain individuals looking toward the recovery of the lands sold by the Indians, or otherwise parted with, under the Canandaigua treaty. Various attempts have been made to advance this contention as a legitimate claim, upon the ground that the Canandaigua

Plate 24. The ratification of the Canandaigua Treaty, proclaimed by George Washington and attested by Edmond Randolph. This is from the copy long owned by the Seneca Nation.

Treaty was not ratified (as a footnote in Kapler's Laws and Treaties would seem to indicate), and that the several Treaties of land sale by Morris and others were not approved by Congress.

Canandaigua Treaty Was Ratified. The Canandaigua Treaty was ratified by the Senate on January 21, 1795, and an attestation of its ratification sent to the Seneca Indians, who for many years kept the copy. It may still be in the archives of the nation, for several years ago it was photographed as shown in the accompanying plate. If the lawyers who are trying to stir up the Seneca to institute a claim can have their way, the Canandaigua Treaty will be nullified, and a return made to the Fort Stanwix Treaty,—thereby giving the Iroquois a large portion of the state as a basis for a suit to obtain possession or compensation.

The truth is that there is no valid claim, though agents are going about on the various reservations and collecting money from individuals. This money, of course, will all go to those who collect it, and their principals, and will not be used in a valid suit which will bring profit to the Seneca or any other Indians, save those who do the "collecting". Thus, based upon the old feeling about the treaties, the Indians are being drained of funds to promote an impossible quest.

The land sales in western New York were made in good faith by both Indians and whites. The Seneca never raised a question as to their validity, and even now the Seneca Nation officially has repudiated the "claim," and refused to listen to the insinuating agents. This led to a movement whereby the proponents of the claim have declared themselves constitutors of the nation, and raised up chiefs of their own, so that under cover of the ancient status, the claim may be made to seem legitimate.

Many factors militate against the success of such a movement. First, the Canandaigua Treaty, so far as it describes the land holdings is concerned, is valid and holden; second, the land sales were and are regarded by the United States as valid, and if by any technicality there should be an error, Congress would immediately validate the title.

10. Modern Conditions.

The Seneca Nation Today. The Seneca Nation of New York Indians is a body of Indians under a republican form of government. It has a President, Secretary, and a Treasurer, and a Board of Eight Councilmen from each reservation. It holds election every two years, and shifts its place of meeting on alternate years from the Court House near Iroquois on the Cattaraugus reservation, to Shongo on the Alleghany.

Some of its prominent public men since the fifties have been Dr. Peter Wilson, Nathaniel T. Strong, Charles Dennis, Sylvester Lay, Rev. Henry Silverheels, Solomon Obail, William Nephew, Henry Stevens, Stephen York, Daniel Twoguns, David George, Edward Cornplanter, Delos Kettle, Job King, Chauncey Jimeson, Henry Pierce, William Hoag, Walter B. Kennedy, Albert Jimerson, Sylvester Crouse, Marvin Crouse, Frank Patterson, William Tallchief, Thomas Kennedy, John Kennedy, etc.

Origin of Modern Names. Soon after the Revolution the Seneca began to establish commercial relations with the whites about them and for this reason stable surnames became a necessity. It was also necessary to have such names in order to lighten the work of paying annuities and listing families. The Indian names were too cumbersome for the settlers to use. Thus, while the Seneca kept their hereditary names, they began to adopt European names from various sources.

Missionaries frequently assisted in selecting names, certain native names were shortened or translated. White friends often "exchanged" names, and half-breed children naturally took the names of their white fathers. To illustrate these statements; the Blacksquirrel family took the name Bishop, from a woman missionary; the Blacksnakes took an older Seneca name and translated it Nephew; one Allegany family adopted the name of one of their captives when they set him free, and so became the Parkers; the Hemlocks and Longfingers simply translated their Indian names. The Shongos and Kenjocketys "Anglicized" their names from older native originals. The translated names of Cornplanter, Big Kettle, Jacket, Green Blanket, Two Guns, Black Chief, and others came down without further change. The Hares, the Hoags, the Crouses, the Poudrays, and others reveal their descent from English, German and French settlers who intermarried.

Citizenship. The Seneca people have long contended that they are an independent nationality, having special treaty rights with the United States. During 1924, without the consent of the Seneca, or any other Iroquois nation, Congress passed a bill declaring all Indians citizens. The Seneca officially object to this, believing themselves to be an Elder people, with a history and a nationality antedating the United States. Some of them say that they cannot see how the United States can make them citizens, any more than it can make the inhabitants of Canada or Mexico United States citizens, while living in their respective countries. Still others have long sought citizenship and have enjoyed its privileges and responsibilities for some time.

A New York Indian has no difficulty in acquiring the status of citizenship, if he seeks it.

Civilization. Thus, has the land of the Genesee gone from Indian occupation, and thus have these people faced the losing game of national life. To many a new day has dawned, but for others the sun has forever set. To many the "Indian Way" is the only way for Indians, but for others the "Right Way" is the only way for those who would compete on even terms with all other men. The ocean of civilization has risen around them, their islands are being engulfed. Those who will not climb to modern heights will be lost, but those who face the facts as they are and adjust themselves to the world as it is will live and carry on the blood-streams of the race. There is no economic stability in the old way, and though the new way is more strenuous, those who gird their loins to grapple with it will find the better things of life. Only those who do will gain a true knowledge of their own cultural status and only they will be able to select and preserve the best that lingers in the old traditions.

The Seneca, in common with their kinsmen, have proven the virility of their race. It is a stock that does not easily give way to innovation, nor will it permit itself easily to be displaced. They have had their place in the sun as a distinctive people, and in their body of thought there have been many fine things. With the new economic life engulfing them it is a serious question whether the Seneca can survive by maintaining their native culture. To continue it is a hazardous experiment, but whether it be life or death, *the Seneca should be given the right of personal choice.*

Plate 25. Peter Wilson, M. D., a Cayuga chief who lived among the Seneca (Circa. 1825-1880).

INDEX.

Logan (Mingo chief), 115.
Louis XIV, 54; Joncaire reports to, 93.
Loss and Waste, 86.

Mahikan (Mohikan, Mahican), a tribe, 27.
Maize culture, 72.
Massacres, 123.
Master of Life, 47.
Material Culture, 61, 84.
Men's Duties, 76.
Men's Work, 85.
Migration, of Iroquois, 18.
Mingo, name for broken tribes, 47, 50.
Modern conditions, 156.
Mohawk Indians, attacked by French, 24; place in Confederacy, 29; 39; with Algonkin tribes, 44; complications, 48; English settlements among, 101; repledge loyalty, 109.
Montour, John, 146.
Montreal, council at, 53.
Morris, Robert, purchase of, 139.
Mound Builders, culture, 16.
Murders, of Indians, 113, 114.
Musicians, Seneca, 153.
Mythology, 79.

Names, of clans, 64; personal, 64; modern Seneca, 156-157.
Niagara, Denonville builds fort at, 56; contest for, 93; claims on, 93; controversy about, 94; secured by French, 98; capitulates, 103; tragedy of Devil's Hole at, 107-109; council at, 109.
Neutral Nation, 18; location of, 19; history of, 20; war with, 43; destroyed, 44.
Newtown attacked, 126.
New York Colony, 94.

Ogden land company, 142, 143.
Ohio Algonkin, 15.
Ohio Seneca, 48, 110, 113.
Old Castle, (See Seneca Castle), 116; 124; residents, 147.
Old King, (Old Smoke, Sayenqueraghta), 116; takes command, 123; settles at Buffalo creek, 129.
Onagee (an Indian town), 95.
Oneida, defeat Champlain, 27, 29, 38.

Onondaga, 29, 30; hostages, 39; sachem, 45.
Oriskany, battle of, 122.
Oswego, 100; English flee, 101.

Parker, Michael, tortured, 127.
Parrish, Jasper, 148.
Peace, the Great, 30, 36.
Personal Privacy, 74.
Private ownership, 74.
Petun (the Tobacco Nation), 42.
Phelps, Oliver, purchase of, 134.
Pickering, Col. Timothy, 134; treaty of, 134.
Pollard, Captain, 146.
Pontiac, conspiracy of, 104; surrenders, 109.
Prisoners, adopted, 42.
Purchase, of land, 133.
Pygmies, 76.

Quakers, defend Seneca, 143.

Raids, 35, 37, 44; southern, 51; of French, 54-56.
Ragueneau, Father, 43.
Red Jacket, 130, 134, 136.
Refugees, Huron, 43; Erie, 46.
Religious belief, of Seneca, 76; 81, 83; 89; Freedom, 76.
Reprisals, 37; Iroquois plan, 56; of Iroquois, 58.
Reservations, location of early, 138, 140; life on, 141; modern, 151; population of, 151.
Revolutionary war, first revolt, 119; problems of, 120; battle of Oriskany, 122.
Rique (an Erie town), 46.
Royal grants, 133.

Sacrifice, 86.
Savagery, of Iroquois, 52; of border whites, 112.
Sayenqueraghta, (See Old King), 119; 123, 124.
Spirits, 79.
St. Ignace, 40.
St. Jean, mission of, 42.
St. James, mission of, 35.
St. Joseph, mission of, 42.
St. Louis, mission of, 40.
Scanenaeenrat, surrenders, 40.
Schooling, 75.
Schuyler, Peter, 96.
Schuyler, Philip, 130.
Seneca Indians, reaction on history, 9; homeland of, 13;